Law ~~Basics~~

FAMILY

SECOND EDITION

*Law*Basics

FAMILY

SECOND EDITION

By

Elaine E. Sutherland

Professor of Child and Family, School of Law,
University of Stirling, Scotland
Professor of Law, Lewis and Clark Law School,
Portland, Oregon, USA

W. GREEN

 **THOMSON REUTERS**

Published in 2008 by Thomson Reuters (Legal) Limited
(Registered in England & Wales, Company No 1679046.
Registered Office and address for service:
100 Avenue Road, London NW3 3PF)
trading as W.Green

Reprinted 2011 by CPI Antony Rowe, Chippenham, Wiltshire

ISBN: 978 0 414 01579 1

No natural forests were destroyed to make this product,
only farmed timber was used and replanted.

A CIP catalogue record for this book is available from the British Library

CONTENTS

TABLE OF CASES

1. INTRODUCTION

Family law is a constant presence in everyday life and, often, it touches upon our most profound moral and religious beliefs. Should we "interfere" with nature through, for example, assisted reproduction, abortion or legalising assisted suicide? What is the best setting in which to raise children? Should same-sex relationships be recognised by the legal system and, if so, is same-sex marriage the route to take? How easy should it be to obtain a divorce? There is no unanimity on these issues, and all the law can do is to try to reflect the prevailing view of the majority, while ensuring respect for minority opinion.

Views on how we deal with issues affecting the family are not static and the dynamism of family law is a product of a host of social and economic influences. Everything from the industrial revolution to the advent of the Internet has had an impact. Female suffrage and, later, the women's movement, changed perceptions of the role of women in society. The 1970s saw the first step towards real recognition of children's rights. Bio-scientific advances have given us greater control over issues of life, death and reproduction. In one sense, choice has never been greater, but the choices must often be made in the context of limited resources. Children may have rights, but is there adequate funding to ensure that they have the support to enforce them effectively? Do we provide sufficient assistance to victims of domestic abuse? Is it accurate to say that we support the family and provide for the resolution of family disputes if we do not make the legal system accessible to all through realistic levels of legal aid provision?

Family law is both intensely personal and increasingly international. If you have a legal problem, how the system deals with it may be all that matters to you for the moment. However, family law exists in the context of accommodating everyone who lives in Scotland. In addition, it is influenced by international standards, as expressed in such international instruments as the European Convention on Human Rights and the United Nations Convention on the Rights of the Child. The global and the local dimensions of family law were highlighted in 1998 when the Human Rights Act and the Scotland Act were passed. The Human Rights Act incorporated the European Convention into the legal systems operating in the United Kingdom and human rights challenges are now a central part of domestic law. The Scotland Act devolved legislative and executive power on many issues, including most matters of family law, to the Scottish Parliament. Essentially, Europe reached into Scotland at the same time as we were taking charge of our own affairs.

This dichotomy is nothing new. While international forces have had an impact on Scots family law, it has always finally been something of a local product. Roman law and Canon law may have had considerable influence in the past, but they were usually adapted to Scottish needs. The distinct nature of Scots family law was guaranteed by the Act of Union and, while note has been taken of developments in English law, reform has always been firmly rooted here. As part of the long comparativist tradition of Scots law, when law reform is being considered, we have always looked further afield than our immediate neighbours. In the context of reform of family law, the greatest single contribution over the last 40 years has come from the Scottish Law Commission. Through a process of rigorous research, comparative analysis, considered reflection and extensive consultation, the Commission has been able to recommend specific and comprehensive reforms. Amid modern calls for consolidation or codification, it is worth remembering that it was the Commission that provided a blueprint for a *Child and Family Law Code* as long ago as 1992, in its *Report on Family Law*.

It is important to know where family law has come from and to consider where it may go in the future. However, essential to the latter exercise is an understanding of where it is at the present. Everyone is entitled to have opinions about what family law should seek to achieve, but a student of family law must be much better informed than an armchair critic. This slim volume seeks to make a small contribution to informing students. However, it must be stressed that it is no more than a basic outline of what is important — hence the fact that the series in which it appears is called *LawBasics*. Certainly, *legal advice should not be offered on the basis of this book alone*. Given the fascinating nature of family law, it is anticipated that students will want to read more widely. Indeed, further reading is essential and reference should be made to the sources of family law and the literature.

Sources of family law
Family law can be found in the following:

- Statutes passed by the Scottish and Westminster Parliaments;
- Statutory instruments and other regulations and directions;
- Modern cases;
- Scots common law, including cases and the institutional writers;
- International instruments;
- Cases from the European Court of Justice and the European Court of Human Rights;
- The literature (see below).

The literature: further reading
We are fortunate, indeed, to have such a wealth of excellent publications, ranging from the general to the specific, in the field of family law.

Frequently cited text
In this volume frequent reference will be made to:
E.E. Sutherland, *Child and Family Law*, 2nd edn (W. Green, 2008)

General texts
L. Edwards and A. Griffiths, *Family Law*, 2nd edn (W. Green, 2006)
J.M. Thomson, *Family Law in Scotland*, 5th edn (Tottel, 2006)

Texts on specific aspects

S.A. Bennett, *Divorce in the Sheriff Court*, 7th edn (Barnstoneworth Press, 2005)

A. Cleland and E.E. Sutherland (eds), *Children's Rights in Scotland*, 2nd edn (W. Green, 2001, 3rd edn forthcoming 2009)

A. Cleland, *Child Abuse, Child Protection and the Law*, (W. Green, 2008)

E.M. Clive, *The Law of Husband and Wife in Scotland*, 4th edn (W. Green, 1997);

P.B. MacNeil, *Adoption of Children in Scotland*, 3rd edn (W. Green, 1998, 4th edn forthcoming 2009)

J.K. Mason and G.T. Laurie, *Law and Medical Ethics*, 7th edn (OUP, 2006)

K. McK. Norrie, *Children's Hearings in Scotland*, 2nd edn (W. Green, 2005)

J. Scoular, *Family Dynamics: Contemporary Issues in Family Law,* (Butterworths, 2001)

A.B. Wilkinson and K. McK. Norrie, *The Law of Parent and Child in Scotland*, 2nd edn (W. Green, 1999)

Journals

There are a number of journals devoted to family law, including W. Green's *Family Law Bulletin*, which concentrates on the position in Scotland, and the *Child and Family Law Quarterly*, *Family Law*, the *International Journal of Law, Policy and the Family*, *International Family Law* and the *Journal of Social Welfare and Family Law*, which cover a variety of jurisdictions and disciplines. In addition, many excellent articles are to be found in the general legal journals published in Scotland, including the *Edinburgh Law Review* and the *Juridical Review*. An absolute "must", in terms of an article to read, is E.M. Clive, "Family Law Reform in Scotland: Past, Present and Future", 1989 J.R. 133.

---

2. NATURAL LEGAL PERSONALITY

The legal system recognises two kinds of legal personality, natural personality and juristic personality. Juristic personality is that which attaches to entities owing their existence to the legal system, like limited companies and trade unions, and is not relevant for our present purpose. Natural personality is that which attaches to individual human beings and having legal personality means that a person is recognised by the legal system. Essentially, he or she becomes a "player" as far as the law is concerned. Since individuals are the building blocks of families, how the legal system approaches natural personality is fundamental to understanding family law. In this chapter we will consider the beginning and end of legal personality, since it is at these stages that family members often become involved in difficult decisions. What matters about people between these two points is often tied to attributes of legal personality, like age, and will be discussed, where appropriate, in later chapters.

THE BEGINNING OF LEGAL PERSONALITY

Answering the question, "When does life begin?" depends on one's own moral, religious and political beliefs and, certainly, there is no universally-accepted answer. As a result, the matter falls within the margin of appreciation permitted to states under the European Convention on Human Rights (*Vo v France* (2005)). The Scottish legal system side-steps the debate neatly, by deciding instead when it will begin to attribute legal personality. The general rule is very simple. Legal personality begins when a person is born alive and continues until a person dies. As a general rule, this approach works well. However, there are situations where injustice would result were the legal system to ignore the period prior to a child's birth. For that reason, the general rule is subject to qualification.

The *nasciturus* principle

The oldest qualification to the general rule is found in the Latin maxim, *nasciturus pro iam habetur quotiens de eius commoda agitur*, known, more simply, as the *nasciturus* principle. Essentially, this permits a backdating of legal personality, to take account of events prior to the child's birth, where this will benefit the child. By applying the *nasciturus* principle, posthumous children have been able to inherit property from a deceased parent (*Findlay's Trustees v Findlay* (1886)) and claim damages for a father's death (*Leadbetter v National Coal Board* (1952)). While the cases all relate to deceased fathers, scientific advances mean that a child could now be born after the mother has died and the *nasciturus* principle would apply equally to such cases. One restriction has been placed on the *nasciturus* principle by statute. Where a child is conceived after the genetic father's death, as a result of the implantation of a stored embryo or the use of stored sperm, the child has no succession rights in the father's estate (Human Fertilisation and Embryology Act 1990 s.28(6)(b)).

Ante-natal injury

An important application of the *nasciturus* principle is in the context of ante-natal injury. Where a child is born with disabilities as a result of something that happened before birth, he or she can recover damages for the injuries from the person responsible for them. So, for example, where hospital staff are negligent in delivering a baby and their negligence results in injury, the child will be able to recover damages for his or her injuries. When it examined the question in 1973, the Scottish Law Commission was so confident that this was already the position in Scots law that it believed there was no need to legislate on the matter (*Report on Liability for Antenatal Injury* (1973)). This contrasts with the position in England and Wales where recovery for antenatal injury is governed by statute (Congenital Disabilities (Civil Liability) Act 1976).

Whether the child's mother could be liable for ante-natal injury remains unlitigated, as yet, in Scotland. Clearly, a pregnant woman is in a unique position in relation to the foetus she is carrying and, applying general delictual principles, where she knows or ought to know that something she is doing is likely to cause injury to the foetus and the resulting child, she will be liable. The Scottish Law Commission was in no doubt that such recovery was competent (*Report on Liability for Antenatal Injury* (1973)). The only real case against maternal liability for ante-natal injury lies in public policy. It has been variously argued that to accept such liability would create friction between the child and the mother; that no real benefit would accrue to the child, since any damages would come from the family coffers; that liability would place unreasonable restrictions on the freedom of action of pregnant women; and that it would give foetal rights priority over the rights of women. It has been suggested that some women might seek abortions in order to avoid liability, although there is no evidence to support such a notion. While maternal liability for ante-natal injury has been accepted in other jurisdictions (*Grodin v Grodin* (1981, Mich., USA); *Lynch v Lynch* (1992, NSW, Australia)), acceptance is far from universal (*Stallman v Youngquist* (1985, Ill., USA); *Dobson v Dobson* (1999, Canada)).

Where a child is born alive and thus acquires legal personality, this can have implications for the parents' right to recover damages for the child's subsequent death. The Damages (Scotland) Act 1976 s.1(1) gives certain relatives of a person who died as a result of his or her injuries the right to recover from the person responsible for the injuries. In *Hamilton v Fife Health Board* (1992 and 1993), the parents of a child who died at three days old as a result of negligent delivery procedures were successful in recovering damages. The view was taken in the Outer House that, since there was no possible benefit to the deceased child, the *nasciturus* principle could not apply. On appeal, the decision was reversed by the Inner House, where the court proceeded on the basis that the child's right to raise an action had accrued when the child was born alive and that the parents, as relatives, had a right to recover under the 1976 Act. In taking the view that it was not necessary to apply the *nasciturus* principle in order to achieve this result, the court was following an earlier Outer House decision (*McWilliams v Lord Advocate* (1992)) where recovery was allowed in similar circumstances without resort to the *nasciturus* principle.

Recognition and regulation of the ante-natal environment
Child protection legislation recognises the ante-natal situation in looking at prior parental conduct when considering whether a child born today may be at risk. Any prior behaviour may be relevant including parental treatment of a previous child and the mother's conduct while she was pregnant. It is competent for the local authority to seek a child protection order in respect of a child where the child has never lived with the parents, but where their past conduct suggests that the child is likely to suffer significant harm and that the order is necessary to protect the child. The case will then be referred

to the Principal Reporter who may arrange a children's hearing (see Chs 6 and 7).

Recognition of the ante-natal environment raises the question of regulating that environment. Clearly, the birth of healthy children is a desirable goal and the state accepts a responsibility to serve that goal by providing ante-natal health care and parental education. Whether the legal system should go further, by, for example, incarcerating pregnant women who persist in drug abuse, has been hotly debated in other jurisdictions. To date, the Scottish courts have not had the opportunity to address the issue of whether a competent, conscious woman should be compelled to undergo a Caesarean delivery against her wishes. Since the general principle is that the consent of a competent patient is a prerequisite to medical treatment, it is thought that the courts would not order such a procedure to be carried out. While courts in other jurisdictions have sanctioned Caesarean deliveries in the face of maternal opposition (*Re S (adult: refusal of medical treatment)* (1992, England); *Jefferson Griffin Spalding County Hospital Authority* (1981, Ga., USA)), the tide appears to have turned against such an invasive approach (*St George's Healthcare National Health Service Trust v S (No. 2)* (1998, England); *Baby Boy Doe v Mother Doe* (1994, Ill., USA)).

The ante-natal period may be relevant for the purpose of criminal law. While, as a general rule, murder and culpable homicide can only be committed in respect of a living person, a charge of murder is competent where the child was still partially inside the mother's body at the time of the alleged offence (*H.M. Advocate v Scott* (1892)). Destruction of a non-viable foetus in the womb will normally amount to abortion and, unless performed within the permitted parameters, will constitute an offence. Where injury is inflicted on the foetus or pregnant woman and the child, subsequently born alive, dies as a result of these injuries, criminal responsibility will attach. Thus, the driver of a car which collided with another vehicle in which a pregnant woman was the passenger was convicted of causing death by reckless driving, when the baby died the following day as a result of injuries sustained in the collision (*McCluskey v H.M. Advocate* (1989)).

Abortion
Prior to 1967, legally-sanctioned abortion was not generally available in Scotland. Since the passing of the Abortion Act 1967, it is no longer an offence to procure or participate in an abortion in certain circumstances. The 1967 Act has been amended by the Human Fertilisation and Embryology Act 1990. No offence is committed where the abortion is performed by a registered medical practitioner and in a National Health Service hospital or place approved by the Secretary of State, provided that at least one of the conditions set out in section 1(1) of the 1967 Act is satisfied. The conditions are that two registered medical practitioners must have formed the opinion in good faith that:
- Continuation of the pregnancy would involve greater risk to the physical or mental health of the woman or any existing children in her family

than would a termination. Such a termination is only permitted up to the twenty-fourth week of pregnancy.

- ·• The termination is necessary to prevent grave permanent injury to the physical or mental health of the pregnant woman.
- • Continuation of the pregnancy would involve risk to life of the pregnant woman greater than termination.
- • There is substantial risk that if the child was born alive it would suffer from such physical or mental abnormalities as to be seriously handicapped.

The final three conditions are not subject to any time limit. In 2008, the most recent attempts to reduce the time limit in respect of the first condition to 12, 20 or 22 weeks was unsuccessful.

Some health care professionals have a conscientious objection to abortion and section 4 of the 1967 Act excuses them from participating in an abortion unless the treatment is directed at saving the life or health of the pregnant woman.

The decision to seek a termination lies, at first instance, with the pregnant woman, who must satisfy one of the conditions outlined above. In other jurisdictions, it had long been established that the potential father had no standing to prevent the abortion from taking place (*Paton v Trustees of BPAS* (1979, England); *C v S* (1988, England); *Tremblay v Daigle* (1989, Canada)). Surprisingly, it was not until 1997 that the Scottish courts had the opportunity to consider the matter for the first time. In *Kelly v Kelly* (1997), the husband of a pregnant woman sought interdict to prevent his wife having a termination. Given the clear indication from abroad that a husband has no standing to prevent an abortion proceeding, the case was argued on a different, rather ingenious, basis. For Mr Kelly it was argued that a child can claim damages for antenatal injury on the basis of the *nasciturus* principle, that such claims could be made by the child's guardian, that interdict was competent to prevent a wrong occurring, and that he was therefore entitled to seek interdict in the present circumstances (as the potential child's guardian). The Second Division rejected his claim on the basis that, while a living child had a right of action in respect of injuries sustained in the womb, the foetus has no legal personality and, thus, can have no rights which are capable of being protected by interdict. In particular, the court took the view that Scots law confers no right on the foetus to a continued existence in the womb, since such a right would conflict with the woman's right to seek a termination under the 1967 Act. An aggrieved husband in Mr Kelly's situation would almost certainly have grounds for an action of divorce on the basis that his wife's behaviour, in having a termination against his wishes, made it unreasonable to expect him to continue to live with her (Divorce (Scotland) Act 1976 s.1(2)(b)).

The issue of a failed abortion was addressed in *Dow v Tayside University Hospital NHS Trust* (2006), where the operation succeeded in removing only one of the twins the pursuer was carrying, leaving her still pregnant with the other. In the light of *McFarlane* (see below) the case was pursued on the basis of contract rather than delict. The sheriff upheld a plea to the relevancy and dismissed the action on the basis that the patient-doctor relationship was a statutory one, that no separate contractual relationship existed between the parties and that the doctor had not warranted the success of the operation.

Wrongful or "uncovenanted" pregnancy and wrongful birth
The terminology in this area of the law can be confusing, in part, due to inconsistent use in the cases and literature, and the classification adopted here is that of Professor Mason (*The Troubled Pregnancy* (2007), p.4). Some adults decide either that they do not want to have children at all or that their existing family is large enough. They view a sterilisation operation (known as a vasectomy in men) as a more certain option than simply relying on contraception. Despite this, a "wrongful" or "uncovenanted" pregnancy may follow, either because the operation itself was performed negligently or because the patient was not advised to use contraception until the success or otherwise of the operation could be established.

"Wrongful birth" comes about as a result of what Professor Mason describes as "inadequate antenatal management." There, the likelihood of a child being born with disabilities should have been foreseen in the circumstances, as, for example, where pre-conception or ante-natal screening should have revealed the risk of the disability. Essentially, by not being informed of the likely dangers, the mother (and, to some extent, her partner) has been deprived of the opportunity to decide not to attempt to become pregnant or, if pregnant, to opt for a termination.

In either case, the couple (or single woman) may consider an action in delict against the doctor or medical facility involved. A whole body of earlier case law permitted recovery in respect, not only of the mother's pain and suffering, but also for the very substantial costs associated with raising a child (*Emeh v Kensington and Chelsea and Westminster Area Health Authority* (1985); *Thake v Morris* (1986); *Anderson v Forth Valley Health Board* (1998)). The issue of recovering the cost of raising the child returned to centre-stage in *McFarlane v Tayside Health Board*. Recovery was denied in the Outer House (1997) but permitted by the Inner House (1998). Ultimately, the House of Lords (2000) denied recovery for the cost of raising a healthy child. The reasoning of the House of Lords is hardly a model of clarity but, essentially, recovery was denied on the basis that the claim was for pure economic loss, the defender had not assumed the risk of the pursuer's economic interests and allowing recovery would not be "fair, just and reasonable" (*Caparo Industries plc v Dickman* (1990)). Damages remain possible for the costs associated with a child's disabilities (*Parkinson v St James and Seacroft University Hospital NHS Trust* (2001)), but not for costs attributable to the mother's pre-existing condition (*Rees v Darlington Memorial Hospital NHS Trust* (2004)).

Wrongful life
The above claims should be distinguished from the child's claim for "wrongful life", where the child seeks to recover damages in respect of his

or her disabilities on the basis that, had the likelihood of his or her condition been known, he or she would either not have been conceived or would have been aborted while a foetus. Essentially, the child is really arguing that, had all the relevant facts been known, he or she would not have been born at all. With few exceptions (*Curlender v Bio-Science Laboratories* (1980, Cal.), courts in the US have rejected such actions on the basis that they are unwilling to take the view that no life at all would be preferable to life with disabilities, that the measure of damages is impossible to assess, and judicial antipathy towards what might be perceived as promoting abortion (*Gleitman v Cosgrove* (1967, N.Y.); *Crowe v Forum Group Inc.* (1991, Ind.)). The only English case on the point rejected the child's claim on the same grounds (*McKay v Essex Area Health Authority* (1982)) and such actions may now be precluded by statute there (Congenital Disabilities (Civil Liability) Act 1976, s.1(2)(b)). More recently, courts in France (*X v Mutuelle d'Assurance du Corps Sanitaire Française* (2000), known as "the *Perruche* case") and the Netherlands (*X v Y* (2003), known as "the *Molenaar* case") have permitted recovery, although claims by the child are now precluded by statute in France. While the Scottish Law Commission was unwilling to commit itself on the matter (*Report on Liability for Antenatal Injury* (1973)), the courts here have now rejected one such claim, at least in the context of compensation for criminal injury (*P's Curator Bonis v Criminal Injuries Compensation Board* (1997)).

THE END OF LEGAL PERSONALITY

Death
Essentially, legal personality ends at death. The dilemmas surrounding the end of a person's life and, in particular, any medical involvement in that process, attract sincere, strongly-held opinions, which are as polarised as those surrounding the issue of abortion. At the outset, it may be helpful to draw a distinction between withdrawal of medical treatment from a patient (i.e. doing little or nothing) and assisting suicide (i.e. doing something to promote a person's death).

Withdrawal of medical treatment
A patient cannot insist on receiving specific medical treatment (*R (on the application of Burke) v General Medical Council* (2006)). Where a competent, adult patient requests the withdrawal of medical treatment, or requests that treatment should be confined to a specific limited type (e.g. relief of pain), there is no legal problem. Treatment of an adult against his or her wishes normally constitutes an assault and, once the patient's views are known, they must be respected.

Where the patient is no longer competent, the decision on treatment must be made by someone else. In the past, courts were willing to consider evidence of "what the patient would have wanted", in terms of life-sustaining treatment. As a result of the recommendations of the Scottish Law Commission (*Report on Incapable Adults* (1995), paras 5.41–5.59), the law has been amended but not wholly in line with the Commission's recommendations. The Adults with Incapacity (Scotland) Act 2000, s.16, enables a competent person to execute a welfare power of attorney, appointing a proxy decision-maker to exercise that power in the event of the grantor's incapacity. The attorney is obliged to take account of the past and present wishes of the adult concerned (s.1(4)(a)). Where the attorney and medical personnel disagree over treatment, the physician may ask the Mental Welfare Commission to nominate a practitioner from a list it keeps (s.50(4) and (9)). If the nominated medical practitioner agrees with the first physician, then treatment can go ahead (s.50(5)). If the nominated practitioner disagrees with the first physician, the latter or anyone with an interest in the patient's welfare may appeal the matter to the Court of Session (s.50(6)) and, again, the court must take account of the past and present wishes of the adult concerned (s.1(4)(a)). Pending the Court's decision, the disputed treatment is not to be given unless it is authorised "by any other enactment or rule of law" for the preservation of the patient's life or the prevention of serious deterioration in his or her medical condition (s.50(7)), unless it is specifically prohibited by interdict (s.50(8)).

The paradigm case of an incompetent patient is one who is in a permanent vegetative state (PVS). Until the decision in *Law Hospital NHS Trust v Lord Advocate* (1996) and directions from the Lord Advocate clarified matters, the families and doctors of such patients were in an uncertain legal position when considering how to proceed. In that case, the patient had been in PVS for over four years. The pursuers (the hospital trust) sought declarator that it would not be unlawful for them to discontinue all life-sustaining and medical treatments and to provide only such treatments as would allow her to die peacefully. The Inner House concluded the test in such cases was what would serve the "best interests" of the patient. It explained further that the "best interests" test should be, "viewed negatively, namely, that it is not in the best interests of the patient to be kept alive by artificial means, where the court is satisfied that the diagnosis is so clear and the prognosis so futile that the [patient] has no interest in being kept alive" (at p.517). The case was remitted back to the Lord Ordinary, who pronounced declarator and the patient subsequently died. Of course, that case was relevant only to civil liability. In order to avoid continuing uncertainty with regard to criminal liability, the Lord Advocate issued a policy statement indicating that he would not authorise prosecution of a medical practitioner who withdrew treatment from a patient in PVS provided that the action was taken in good faith and with the authority of the court.

Assisted suicide and euthanasia

Physician-assisted suicide has been legalised in a number of jurisdictions, with the earliest example being the Death with Dignity Act, operating in Oregon, US, since 1998. The Act requires the physician and the patient to comply with a number of, fairly rigorous, conditions before the physician can prescribe a lethal prescription of drugs for the patient to take. Belgium, the Netherlands and Switzerland provide other — and distinctly regulated — examples. However, it seems no state is obliged to take this route, since the European Court of Human Rights has taken the position that article 2 (right to life) of the European Convention does not guarantee any "right to die" (*Pretty v United Kingdom* (2002)).

In Scotland, assisted suicide, regardless of whether the assistance is given by a doctor or someone else, is illegal. Depending on the circumstances, the accused may be charged with murder or culpable homicide and it may be some reflection of the attitude of prosecutors that, even where the original charge is murder, a guilty plea to the lesser charge is often accepted (*H.M. Advocate v Brady* (1997)). In addition, there are cases which illustrate leniency in sentencing where it is accepted that the accused acted out of love or concern for the deceased. However, such decisions are no guarantee that a particular prosecutor or court would take an equally compassionate and lenient attitude in the future. There has been consultation on the possibility of introducing legislation on assisted suicide in the Scottish Parliament (*Dying with Dignity* (2005)), so the position here may change.

Presumption of death
Sometimes, while all the circumstances point to the fact that a person has died, no body can be produced. For example, where a person boarded an aeroplane which crashed into the ocean with no survivors, it is reasonable to assume that the person has died. In addition, the law accepts less dramatic circumstances as indicating death, as for example where a person has been missing for a long period of time and no one comes forward to indicate that the person is alive. The matter has long been regulated by statute and the current legislation is the Presumption of Death (Scotland) Act 1977. An action to have a person declared dead may be brought in either the sheriff court or the Court of Session by any person having an interest (s.1(1)). A declarator is competent in two situations. The first arises where there is a clear indication that a person died at a particular time, as in the case of the passenger on the crashed aeroplane, and the action can be raised immediately after the crash. The second situation arises where the person "has not been known to be alive for a period of at least seven years" and, obviously, such actions may only be raised after that period of time has elapsed. Where it is established that either of the two conditions is satisfied, the court must grant the declarator providing that the person died, in the first case, at a specific date or, in the second case, at the date seven years after the person was last known to be alive.

Once a person has been declared dead, the decree is conclusive on all matters and effective against any person for all civil purposes including any rights in property (s.3). Such a decree terminates the missing person's marriage for all time and the limited provisions allowing for variation or recall of the decree do not revive the marriage (s.4(5)). Only criminal liability is unaffected by a declarator of death. In order to accommodate the possibility that the person declared dead might reappear, the Act contains provision for variation or recall of the decree (s.4). Where the missing person reappears within five years, the court may make such order as is "fair and reasonable in all the circumstances of the case" regulating property rights, but such orders do not affect any rights acquired by a third party in good faith and for value (s.5).

Presumption of survivorship

Where two people die in a common calamity, it may be impossible to ascertain which of them survived the other and the Succession (Scotland) Act 1964 introduced a general presumption that the younger person survives the elder (s.31(1)(b)). However, there are two exceptions to this presumption. First, where the two persons were husband and wife, neither is presumed to survive the other (s.31(1)(a)). This prevents the estates of both of them being inherited by the survivors of only one. The second exception applies where the elder person has left property to the younger, whom failing to a third party. Where the younger person has died intestate, the elder person is presumed to have survived the younger for the purpose of that particular legacy only and the property passes to the third party (s.32). The whole scheme introduced by the 1964 Act applies only in cases of doubt and if it can be established on the balance of probabilities that one person did in fact survive the other, then the usual rules of succession apply (*Lamb v H.M. Advocate* (1976)). For this reason, it is quite common in wills for the testator to provide that a particular beneficiary will only inherit if he or she survives the testator by, for example, 30 days. That ensures either that the beneficiary will enjoy the property or that it will pass to other people chosen by the testator.

Further reading:

E.E. Sutherland, *Child and Family Law*, 2nd edn (W. Green, 2008), Ch.2

J.K. Mason and G.T. Laurie, *Law and Medical Ethics*, 7th edn (OUP, 2006), Chs 5, 6, 13 and 17

J.K. Mason, The Troubled Pregnancy: Legal Wrongs and Rights in Reproduction, (CUP, 2007)

J. Purves, MSP, *Dying with Dignity,* (Scottish Parliament, 2005), available at: *http://www.scottish.parliament.uk/business/bills/pdfs/mb-consultations/DyingWithDignity-report.pdf* [accessed June 24, 2008]

---

3. CHILDREN, PARENTS AND OTHER FAMILY MEMBERS

The latter half of the twentieth century saw enormous changes in the way the legal system viewed children, both in their own right and as family members and legal developments have continued this century. This chapter will examine the emergence of the concept of children's rights and the significance of a child's age, before moving on to look at the way children are regarded as being linked to significant adults, through biological parenthood or the fictions applying to assisted reproduction. It will conclude with a brief word about other family members.

CHILDREN'S RIGHTS

Internationally, children can benefit from rights given to all persons, irrespective of age. So, for example, the European Convention on Human Rights (1950) always applied to children (*Marckx v Belgium* (1968)) and its importance increased throughout the United Kingdom with the passing of the Human Rights Act 1998. A turning point in international recognition of children's rights came in 1989 when the Convention on the Rights of the Child was adopted unanimously by the General Assembly of the United Nations. The United Kingdom ratified the Convention in 1991 and there is no doubt that its provisions have influenced subsequent legislation here – from the Children (Scotland) Act 1995 onwards. The 1995 Act will be examined in more detail in later chapters. However, it is important at this point to be aware of the Act's fundamental principles, sometimes described as the child lawyer's mantra. These apply, with occasional exceptions, throughout child law. They are:

- The welfare of the child is the paramount consideration;
- The child must be given the opportunity to express his or her views and account will be taken of these views in the light of the child's age and maturity;
- The court will not make any order unless to do so will be better than not making the order.

THE SIGNIFICANCE OF AGE

As we have seen, every child acquires legal personality from the moment of birth. However, there are obvious practical reasons why young children cannot be active participants in the legal system. Thus, the law has always recognised that a child cannot acquire legal capacity until a later stage. Since maturity is a very individual matter, the legal system sometimes prefers to link capacity to the readily verifiable fact of chronological age. Age is calculated by regarding a person as reaching a particular age at the beginning of the relevant anniversary of his or her birth (Age of Legal Capacity (Scotland) Act 1991 s.6(1)), i.e. just after midnight on one's birthday. Where a person is born on February 29, the relevant anniversary is March 1 in any year other than a leap year (1991 Act s.6(2)).

The general rule is that a person below the age of 16 has no legal capacity to enter into transactions and that any purported contract is void (1991 Act s.1(1)). If the law left it at that, we would be in the absurd position that a 12-year-old could not contract to buy a bar of chocolate. For this reason, there are a host of exceptions to this general rule and the exceptions are often more important than the rule itself. The exceptions are contained in the 1991 Act, unless otherwise stated, and are as follows:

- *Common transactions.*

Children have the capacity to enter a transaction provided that two conditions are satisfied. First, the transaction itself must be of a kind commonly entered into by persons of the child's age and circumstances and, secondly, the terms of the transaction must not be unreasonable (s.2(1)). This is the most flexible and practically significant of the exceptions to the general rule.

- *Instructing a solicitor in connection with a civil matter.*

A person under the age of 16 has the capacity to instruct a solicitor in connection with a civil matter provided that the child or young person has a general understanding of what it means to do so (s.2(4A)). A child of 12 years or older is presumed to have sufficient understanding, although younger children may qualify. None of this has any bearing on the child's capacity in relation to any criminal matter (s.2(4)(c)).

- *Making a will.*

A young person of 12 years old or over has the capacity to make a will (s.2(2)).

- *Consenting to surgical, dental or medical treatment.*

A person below the age of 16 has the capacity to consent to (almost) any surgical, medical or dental procedure or treatment where the qualified practitioner attending him or her is of the opinion that the young person understands the nature and possible consequences of the procedure or treatment (s.2(4)). An exception prevents a person under the age of 16 from being a live organ donor, albeit a person of 12 or over can consent to post-mortem use of his or her organs (Human Tissue (Scotland) Act 2006 ss.8 and 17).

- *Parental responsibilities and rights.*

While parental responsibilities and rights are usually held in respect of a person under 16, such young people may themselves be parents. Where this happens, the young parent may hold parental responsibilities and rights in respect of his or her own child (s.1(3)(g)).

- *Consenting to adoption.*

A young person of 12 years old or over has the right to consent to, or veto, his or her own adoption except where he or she is incapable of consenting (Adoption and Children (Scotland) Act 2007 s.32).

- *Consenting to a permanence order.*

A young person of 12 years old or over has the right to consent to, or veto, the granting of a permanence order being made in respect of him or her, again, except where he or she is incapable of consenting (Adoption and Children (Scotland) Act 2007 s.84).

- *Transactions entered into before the commencement of the Act.*

Where the transaction was entered into before the 1991 Act came into force on September 25, 1991, the common law rules will apply (s.1(3)(a)).

- *Other matters not affected.*

While the 1991 Act supersedes all prior legislation governing the capacity of young people (s.1(4)), it makes clear that its provisions do not affect certain other matters. Thus, legislation laying down age limits expressed in years remains valid (s.1(3)(d)). Delictual liability and criminal responsibility remain unaffected by the Act (s.1(3)(c)).

Young people over the age of 16 have full legal capacity to enter into any transaction (s.1(1)(b)). However, the 1991 Act recognises that these "beginners", in terms of exercising capacity, may need some additional protection from their own inexperience and greater vulnerability to exploitation. It allows a person under the age of 21 to apply to the court to have a transaction which he or she entered into while between the ages of 16 and 18 set aside (s.3(1)). In order to mount a successful challenge, the young person must demonstrate that the transaction was a "prejudicial transaction", defined in terms of two criteria. First, it must be shown that the transaction was one which an adult, exercising reasonable prudence, would not have entered into in the circumstances at the time (s.3(2)(a)). Secondly, it must be shown that the transaction itself has caused, or is likely to cause, substantial prejudice to the young person (s.3(2)(b)).

Regardless of their impact on the young person, certain transactions and other activities are explicitly exempted from applications for reduction under the Act. It should be remembered that this does not bar applications for reduction on the many other grounds available to anyone, irrespective of age, including misrepresentation, fraud, and coercion. The following cannot be challenged under the 1991 Act:

- Making a will;
- Consent to adoption;
- Action taken in the course of civil proceedings;
- Consent to any surgical, medical or dental procedure;
- A transaction entered into by the young person in the course of his or her trade, occupation or profession;
- A transaction where a young person has induced the other party to enter it by fraudulent misrepresentation as to his or her age or any other material fact;
- A transaction which the young person has ratified after reaching the age of 18, knowing that it could be set aside;
- A transaction which has been given prior approval by a court on the application of all of the parties to it, including the young person (s.3(3)).

Age in other contexts

The 1991 Act specifically excludes delict and the criminal law from its ambit and does not affect age-related restrictions found in other statutes (s.1(3)). A child may claim damages in delict from any age and the child's parents are not placed in any special position, in this respect, since a child can sue his or her parents (*Young v Rankin* (1934)). The fact that a pursuer in an action founded on delict is a child does become relevant, however, in the context of contributory negligence: that is, when the defender argues that the harm was caused, at least in part, by the child's own conduct. The child's behaviour here is assessed in the light of that child's age and experience and, thus, a child of five, living in an urban environment, can be expected to have some appreciation of the dangers of traffic (*McKinnell v White* (1971)). There is no minimum age for delictual liability in Scotland. Where the parent instigates the child's delictual act or has been negligent in, for example, failing to supervise the child, liability may attach to the parent. However, parents have no automatic responsibility for the delictual acts of their children.

Scots law attributes criminal responsibility from the age of eight years old and Scotland has one of the lowest ages for criminal responsibility in the world. Where a child is alleged to have committed an offence, he or she will almost always be dealt with in the children's hearing system which adopts a treatment-based approach to the child's problems (see Ch.7). However, prosecution of children in the criminal courts is provided for in a limited range of circumstances, on the instructions of the Lord Advocate (Criminal Procedure (Scotland) Act 1995 s.42). Where convicted, the child can be sentenced by the court, although provision is made for involving the children's hearing system in sentencing. This involvement does not apply to cases where the penalty for the case is fixed by law and, thus, a child convicted of murder will not benefit from the provision. A whole range of offences may only be committed against a child below a specific age.

An enormous number of statutory age-related restrictions exist. Since they were introduced at different times and, sometimes, as a quick response to a particular burning issue of the day, the result has been described as "a badly designed mosaic". The rationale behind age-related restrictions is often to protect children from perceived dangers of the adult world. Thus, the attempt is made to deny children below a particular age access to tobacco (18 years old), alcohol (18) and gambling (18, except the National Lottery, where 16 is the age limit). Sometimes the desire is to protect the community as well as children, hence restrictions on driving (16–21 years old, depending on the type of vehicle) and possessing air-rifles and firearms (14–17 years old, depending on the type of weapon and the offence charged). On other occasions, the law appears to be offering guidance on what might be described as "good parenting". This would explain legislation which prohibits giving alcohol to a child below the age of five, except for medical purposes.

PARENTAGE

As we shall see, the fact of being a child's parent may be important for a whole range of purposes. Mothers, married fathers and many non-marital fathers acquire parental responsibilities and parental rights automatically. Parental consent is normally required before a child can be adopted, thus, establishing the child-parent link is important. In addition, sight should not be lost of the social and psychological importance of knowing about parentage as part of one's identity. Of course, in most cases, the matter is uncontentious. We will look first at parentage in the "traditional" setting before moving on to reproductive technology and its implications for parentage.

Maternity
Disputes over the maternity of a child are rare, although not unknown, as evidenced by *Douglas v Duke of Hamilton* (1769). Maternity may be important for immigration purposes and the advent of DNA profiling has been of assistance in resolving disputed cases in this context. Cases have arisen in other jurisdictions where it has been alleged that, due to an error at the hospital, two women have gone home with each other's baby, the mistake being discovered at a later stage (*Twigg v Mays* (1989 and 1993) (USA)), with the resulting dispute being over both the maternity and the paternity of the children.

Paternity
Paternity disputes have long been a feature of the legal system and section 5 of the Law Reform (Parent and Child) (Scotland) Act 1986 contains a number of presumptions to assist the courts in disputed cases. These presumptions merely provide a legal starting point and all of them are rebuttable: that is, they can be displaced by proof on the balance of probabilities (s.5(4)). A man is presumed to be the father of a child in the following circumstances:
- If he was married to the child's mother at any time from the child's conception to his or her birth (s.5(1)(a)). This presumption applies to all kinds of marriage and regular, irregular, void and voidable marriages are all sufficient to trigger its application (s.5(2));
- Where the above provision does not apply, if both he and the mother have acknowledged that he is the father and he has been registered as such (s.5(1)(b));
- Where the court has declared him to be the father of a child (s. 5(3)). As we will see, the court can grant declarator of parentage; that is, it can declare that a particular man is a child's father. Such a declarator will be presumed to be accurate unless displaced by a later successful challenge.

Establishing parentage or non-parentage
While disputes over a child's parentage are almost always about paternity, rather than maternity, the same procedure applies in either case. An action for declarator of parentage or non-parentage may be raised in either the Court of Session or the sheriff court (1986 Act s.7(1)) and parentage may also be determined incidentally to other proceedings (s.7(5)). The action may be raised by anyone with an interest, including, of course, the child, although most actions are raised by mothers seeking to establish paternity. In order to rebut any of the presumptions discussed above, the pursuer must prove his or her case on the balance of probabilities (s.5(4)). The court must be satisfied as to the sufficiency of evidence (Civil Evidence (Scotland) Act 1988 s.8(1)), but corroborated evidence is no longer required (1988 Act s.1(1)).

The most commonly-used evidence relies on DNA profiling, which makes it possible to establish that a person is the father of a child. Since DNA profiling requires the taking of a sample of blood or other body tissue from the parties involved, it raises the issue of consent to testing. While a civil court cannot compel a competent adult to submit to such a test (*Whitehall v Whitehall* (1958); *Torrie v Turner* (1990)), the court may request a party to the proceedings to do so and draw any adverse inference it considers appropriate from refusal (Law Reform (Miscellaneous (Provisions) (Scotland) Act 1990 s.70). This does not mean that the pursuer will automatically succeed in establishing paternity (*Smith v Greenhill* (1994)), but it does reduce the incentive simply to keep one's head down. A sample will also be required from the child. Where he or she is of sufficient age and understanding to appreciate what is involved in the test and the likely consequences, the child can consent (Age of Legal Capacity (Scotland) Act 1991 s.2(4)), but, in most cases, children are too young to give consent. Any person who has parental responsibilities in respect of the child under 16 or care and control of him or her may consent on the child's behalf (1986 Act s.6(2)). As we shall see, this creates an obstacle to a non-marital father seeking to establish paternity if the child's mother will not consent to testing of a young child (Ch.5, below). The court may consent to samples being taken from "any person who is incapable of giving consent" in two situations (1986 Act s.6(3)). The first is where there is no one entitled to give consent and the second is where there is such a person but, either it is not reasonably practicable to obtain that person's consent, or that person is unwilling to accept the responsibility of giving or withholding consent. The court is prohibited from consenting to the taking of a sample unless it is satisfied that the taking of the sample "would not be detrimental to the person's health" (1986 Act s.6(4)).

Where the samples necessary for DNA profiling cannot be obtained, other forms of evidence will be relevant. For example, evidence of an established relationship between the child's mother and the alleged father might support attributing paternity to him, while evidence of the gestation period (the time between conception and birth) has been used to suggest that a particular man could not be the father of the child. Evidence of a physical resemblance between the child and the alleged father is not generally accepted by courts (*S v S* (1977); cf. *Grant v Countess of Seafield* (1926)).

"Abolition" of illegitimacy

Historically and like many other legal systems, Scots law distinguished "legitimate" children, whose parents were or had been married to each other, from those who were "illegitimate". Statute intervened to reduce the negative impact on children of the distinction (e.g. Bastards (Scotland) Act 1836, Law Reform (Parent and Child) (Scotland) Act 1986). The most recent amendment to the law is found in the Family Law (Scotland) Act 2006, section 21, which provides that "no person whose status is governed by Scots law shall be illegitimate." Thus, equality for (almost) all Scottish children has been achieved, irrespective of parental marital status, although the amendment has no effect on the transmission of titles and honours (Law

Reform (Parent and Child) (Scotland) Act 1986 s.9(1)(c)). Nor does it place all fathers on an equal footing in terms of acquiring parental responsibilities and parental rights (see Ch.5).

ASSISTED REPRODUCTION

Enormous scientific advances have been made in the field of assisted reproduction and individuals and couples who are experiencing difficulty in having a child can now be helped through a range of treatment options. The *Report of the Committee of Inquiry into Human Fertilisation and Embryology* (Warnock Report) (1984) attempted to address the ethical and legal dilemmas surrounding the techniques. It resulted in the Human Fertilisation and Embryology Act 1990 which provides for the regulation of fertility services, usually through the Human Fertilisation and Embryology Authority (HFEA), and for rules on determining parentage. The Human Fertilisation and Embryology Bill (2007 HL Bill 6, 2008 HC Bill 80), currently proceeding through Westminster, will make some significant changes to the law here. We will look briefly at the techniques available before considering the rules on parentage which apply to children who result from them.

The techniques

Donor insemination (D.I.)
D.I. is the process whereby semen obtained from a (usually anonymous) donor is injected into the woman's uterus. If fertilisation occurs, the resulting pregnancy proceeds in the usual way. For a married or different-sex cohabiting couple who are experiencing difficulty in having a child due to the male partner's infertility, donor insemination is a relatively simple way for them to have a child who is biologically linked to the woman. It should be noted that donor insemination does not constitute adultery for the purpose of divorce (*McLennan v McLennan* (1958)). Were a wife to undergo donor insemination without her husband's consent, her distressed husband could probably obtain a divorce on the basis that her action made it unreasonable to expect him to live with her (Divorce (Scotland) Act 1976 s.1(2)(b)). For single women, DI provides an avenue to parenthood without the need for sexual intercourse. DI offers female couples the opportunity to have a child whom the couple can raise together, in a practical sense and, if the reforms contained in the Human Fertilisation and Embryology Bill become law, dual legal parenthood will also be possible.

Partner insemination (P.I.)
The technique for P.I. is the same as that for D.I., save that the donor is the woman's partner. Controversy surrounded the decision of the Court of Appeal in *R v Human Fertilisation and Embryology Authority, ex p. Blood* (1997), where a widow was successful in gaining permission to use her deceased husband's semen and, ultimately, had their children. The semen had been removed while he was in a coma and, since he had no opportunity to give his consent to its use after his death, the 1990 Act prevented such

use in the United Kingdom (Sch.3, para.2(2)). However, the court felt bound by European law to permit its export to Belgium where the widow obtained treatment. Further litigation followed, resulting in legislation dealing with registering the paternity of post-mortem P.I. children (see below).

In vitro fertilisation (IVF)
IVF involves the fertilisation of the ovum in laboratory conditions and the transfer of the resulting embryo into the uterus. The ovum may have come from the woman into whom the embryo is implanted or from a donor. The fertilising sperm may have come from her partner, if she has one, or a donor. The gamete contributors must consent the storage and use of the resulting embryos and may withdraw consent prior to implantation (Sch.3; *Evans v Amicus Healthcare Ltd.* (2004); *Evans v United Kingdom* (2006)). It was in the context of IVF that one of the most spectacular cases of an error occurred when a woman was implanted with the "wrong" embryos (*L Teaching Hospital NHS Trust v A* (2003)).

Surrogacy
There are numerous different scenarios that can lead to what is described as "surrogacy". What is known as "full surrogacy" involves a woman ("the surrogate") agreeing to carry a foetus, produced from the gametes (sperm and ovum) obtained from a couple ("the commissioning couple"), with the intention that the child will be handed over to the couple to be raised by them as their child. "Partial surrogacy" may involve sperm donated by the husband of the commissioning couple being used to fertilise the surrogate's own ovum. Surrogacy has attracted more controversy than other techniques used to assist in reproduction, partly because of the greater degree of active involvement of a third party, and partly because of the commercialism associated with it. The Surrogacy Arrangements Act 1985 was passed to address the second concern. It makes it an offence to negotiate a surrogacy arrangement on a commercial basis (ss.1(8) and 2(3)) or to be involved in advertising such arrangements (s.3) and renders surrogacy agreements unenforceable (s.1A).

Parentage
The 1990 Act provides a number of rules on the parentage of children produced as a result of assisted reproduction. It should be noted that these are fixed rules and, unlike the presumptions of paternity, discussed above, cannot be rebutted. Where a person is to be treated as the mother or father of a child as a result of the Act, the effect is stated to apply "for all purposes" (s.29(1)), although it does not apply to the transmission of any title, coat of arms, honour or dignity (s.29(5)(a)).

Maternity
Where a woman is carrying, or has carried, a child as a result of an embryo or sperm and eggs being placed in her, that woman and no other woman is to be treated as the mother of the child (s.27(1)). There are two ways by

which the carrying woman can be displaced as the child's mother. The first is where the child is adopted by the ordinary method of adoption whereby the adopters take over as the child's parents and the child's legal link with birth relatives is severed (s.27(3)). The second is through the special provision, introduced by the 1990 Act and confined to surrogacy, whereby the couple who commissioned a surrogate to carry a foetus, genetically linked to one or both of the couple, can apply for a special kind of parental order (s.30). This parental order is, effectively, a form of accelerated adoption and is discussed below.

Paternity
The provision dealing with paternity is a little more complicated than that on maternity. It applies not only where a child is being or has been carried by a woman as a result of an embryo, or sperm and eggs being placed in her, but also where the woman has been inseminated artificially (s.28(1)). Where the woman was married at the time of the treatment but the embryo was created using sperm from someone other than her husband, her husband is treated as the child's father unless it can be shown that he did not agree to the treatment (s.28(2)). Thus, the onus is placed firmly on the husband to rebut consent. Where no man would be treated as the child's father by the application of the provision dealing with husbands, discussed above, the woman's male partner will be treated as the child's father, provided that both of the following conditions are met:
- The man and woman are treated together;
- In the course of treatment services are provided by a person who is licensed to provide such services (s.28(3)).

In either case, no other man is treated as the child's father (s.28(4)). "Do-it-yourself" D.I., where a woman obtains semen and inseminates herself without using a licensed provider, does not attract the protection of the Act and the donor remains the child's legal father (*X v Y (Parental Rights: Insemination)* (2002)). At present, the 1990 Act creates the fiction of parentage for the mother's male partner only. The Human Fertilisation and Embryology Bill contains provisions to amend the law for male partners and create an equivalent opportunity for the mother's female partner to be treated as the child's second parent. Having secured the right to use her deceased husband's sperm to have two children (*R v Human Fertilisation and Embryology Authority, ex p. Blood* (1997), above), the law as it stood did not permit his name to appear as their father on their birth certificates. Ms Blood raised another court action in respect of this issue, the authorities withdrew their opposition and the Human Fertilisation and Embryology (Deceased Fathers) Act 2003 was passed, permitting such registration where the deceased father has consented to post-mortem use of his sperm.

Parental orders
Mention has been made of the special provision for the making of a parental order in favour of gametes donors, essentially an order which is similar to an adoption order (1990 Act s.30). Such an order is available only where a

host of conditions are satisfied and is, in any event, at the discretion of the court. The conditions are as follows:

- The application must be made by a married couple;
- The child concerned must have been carried by a woman other than the wife as a result of the placing in her of an embryo or sperm and eggs or her artificial insemination;
- The gametes of the husband or the wife, or both, were used to bring about the creation of the embryo;
- The couple must apply for the order within six months of the child's birth;
- The child's home must be with the couple both at the time of the application and at the time of the order being made;
- The husband or the wife, or both, must be domiciled in the United Kingdom or in the Channel Islands or the Isle of Man at the time of the application and at the time of the order being made;
- Both the husband and the wife must have attained the age of 18 by the time any order is made;
- Both the woman who carried the child and the father of the child (including a man treated as such by virtue of section 28 of the Act) have freely, and with full understanding of what is involved, agreed unconditionally to the making of the order;
- The court must be satisfied that no money or other benefit (other than for expenses reasonably incurred) has been given or received by the husband or the wife for: the making of the order, any agreement required, the handing over of the child to them, or the making of any arrangements with a view to the making of the order.

At present, parental orders are available only to married couples. The Human Fertilisation and Embryology Bill, if passed, would amend the 1990 Act to extend them to civil partners and cohabiting couples "living as partners in an enduring family relationship".

OTHER FAMILY MEMBERS
Clearly, a child will often have many other relatives including siblings, aunts and uncles and grandparents. These relationships are of significance for the law on incest, prohibited degrees for marriage and civil partnership registration and succession. However, none of these individuals acquire parental responsibilities or parental rights in respect of a child automatically. When the Family Law (Scotland) Act 2006 was going through the Scottish Parliament, a vocal grandparents lobby was unsuccessful when it sought to secure for grandparents an automatic right of contact with a grandchild. A sop was thrown to them in the form of the Charter for Grandchildren, a statement of ideals (of no legal effect) about the importance of grandparents in a child's life. The grandparents lobby has used the Public Petitions procedure in its attempt to give the Charter teeth by having it made legally binding (PE 1051), so far without success. Step-parents do not acquire parental responsibilities or parental rights

automatically, although they become liable to aliment a child they have accepted as a member of their family (see Ch.5).

Further reading:
E.E. Sutherland, *Child and Family Law*, 2nd edn (W. Green, 2008), Chs 3, 4 and 7
A. Cleland and E.E. Sutherland (eds), *Children's Rights in Scotland*, 2nd edn (W. Green, 2001, 3rd edn forthcoming 2009)
J.K. Mason and G.T. Laurie, *Law and Medical Ethics*, 7th edn (OUP, 2006), Ch.4.

---

4. ADOPTION

Adoption is the creation of the child-parent relationship by order of the court (*J and J v C's Tutor* (1948), per Lord President Cooper, p.641). The concept came to Scots law comparatively late, in 1930. Typically, it provided for a single mother, who felt unable to raise her child, handing the child over, via an agency, to a married couple. The adoption setting has changed dramatically since these early days. Few adoptions now involve babies and the children being adopted are often older. About one third of all adoptions are step-parent adoptions; that is, adoption by a parent's new husband or wife, with the child living with the parent and new spouse. There was already disquiet over whether aspects of adoption law were human right compliant (*West Lothian Council v M* (2002); *G v City of Edinburgh Council* (2002)), when an extensive review was undertaken by the Adoption Policy Review Group, culminating in its report, *Better Choices for Our Children* (2005). Many of the report's recommendations were implemented in the Adoption and Children (Scotland) Act 2007, and references are to that Act unless otherwise stated. While the 2007 Act is not in force at the time of writing, this chapter is written as if it were.

THE PURPOSE OF MODERN ADOPTION LAW
Whatever benefits adoption may bring to the adults involved, the child's interests are the focal point of adoption and the fundamental principles of child law apply.

Paramountcy of the child's welfare
In any decision relating to the adoption of a child, the court or the adoption agency is directed to "regard the need to safeguard and promote the welfare of the child throughout the child's life as the paramount consideration" (s.14(3)). All the circumstances of the case must be taken into account (s.14(2)), but the court or agency must have regard, "in particular", to the value of a stable family unit in the child's development; the child's

ascertainable views regarding the decision (taking account of the child's age and maturity); the child's religious persuasion, racial origin and cultural and linguistic background; and the likely effect, throughout the child's life, of making an adoption order (s.14(4)). In addition, the court or the agency need simply "have regard" to the views of the parents, guardians and other relatives of the child (s.14(5)).

The child's views
In addition to taking account of the child's views (s.14(4)), a child of 12 years old and over has the right to veto or consent to his or her own adoption unless he or she is incapable of doing so (s.32(1)).

No unnecessary/non-beneficial orders
In the context of adoption, this principle is articulated in three distinct ways. First, "before making any arrangements for the adoption of a child" the adoption agency must "consider whether adoption is likely best to meet the needs of the child or whether there is some better practical alternative for the child" and, if such an alternative is present, then the agency is directed not to make arrangements for adoption (s.14(6) and (7)). Secondly, where the court is considering making a permanence order (which may, but need not, authorise the child's adoption), it is directed not to grant the order unless "it would be better for the child that the order be made than that it should not be made." (s.84(3)). Thirdly, a court must not make an adoption order unless it would be better for the child that the order be made than not (s.28(2))

THE PARTIES INVOLVED IN ADOPTION

Who may be adopted?
Any person under the age of 18 who has never been a spouse or a civil partner may be adopted (s.28(7)) and an adopted child may be the subject of a subsequent adoption order (s.28(6)). Provided that the proceedings began before the child's eighteenth birthday, the petition can be granted after he or she reaches 18 (s.28(4)).

Who may adopt?
Until recently, Scots law permitted adoption by a single person or a married (by definition, different-sex) couple only and broadening the range of prospective adopters was probably the most controversial reform contained in the 2007 Act (see also, *Fretté v France* (2004) and *E.B. v France* (2008)). The following may now apply to adopt a child:

- *A "relevant couple"*
A relevant couple consists of spouses, civil partners or two people living together "in an enduring family relationship" as if they were spouses or civil partners(s.29(3)).

- *One person alone*

A single person may adopt a child. Where a person has a partner, he or she remains eligible to adopt alone provided that his or her spouse or civil partner cannot be found, or that the couple have separated and are living apart with the likelihood that the separation will be permanent, or his or her spouse or civil partner is incapable, by reason of ill-health (whether physical or mental) of making an application for an adoption order (s.30(4)). A similar ill-health provision applies to cohabiting couples (s.30(5)).

- *The child's parent*

Adoption by a child's birth parent is now a rarity and is permitted only where the other parent is dead or cannot be found, or, by virtue of section 28 of the Human Fertilisation and Embryology Act 1990, there is no other parent, or there is some other reason justifying the exclusion of that other parent (s.30(7)).

- *The child's step-parent*

The increase in step-families has resulted in an increase in step-parent adoption. The step-parent applying to adopt must be part of a relevant couple with the child's parent and the latter must be at least 18 years old (s.30(3)). A difficulty with step-parent adoptions has always been that, once the adoption takes place, it severs the child's legal link with the "other" birth parent (i.e. the birth parent who is not part of a relevant couple with the step-parent) and that parent's relatives. Where the "other" parent is opposed to the step-parent's adoption of a child, the court may dispense with that parent's consent, but it will not do so lightly (*A v B* (1987) and *AB and CD v EF* (1991)). It may be that extending parental responsibilities and parental rights to the step-parent is a better practical alternative to adoption.

In addition to the above requirements, applicants for adoption must be at least 21 years old (ss.29(1)(a) and 30(1)(a)). Where one person is applying to adopt a child alone, he or she must be domiciled in a part of the British Isles or have been so resident for at least a year immediately prior to the application (s.30(1)(c) and (6)). Where two people apply to adopt a child together, one of them must be so domiciled or the couple must have been so resident for at least a year immediately prior to their application (s.29(2)). It will be remembered that there is a form of expedited adoption – parental orders – available in the surrogacy context and it is subject to its own rules (see Ch.3).

THE AGREEMENT OF THE CHILD'S PARENTS AND GUARDIANS

Parents and guardians

The starting point in adoption is that each parent and guardian of the child "understands what the effect of making of an adoption order would be and consents to the making of the order" (s.31(2)(a)). The consent of the child's mother is ineffective if given less than six weeks after the child's birth (s.31(11)). "Parent", for this purpose, means, "(a) a parent who has any parental responsibilities or parental rights in relation to the child, or (b) a parent who, by virtue of permanence order which does not include provisions granting authority for the child to be adopted, has no such parental responsibilities or rights" (s.31(15)). As we shall see (Ch.5), a non-marital father only acquires parental responsibilities and parental rights automatically if he registered his paternity on or after 4 May 2006. Unless he has acquired these rights or responsibilities by agreement with the child's mother or from a court, a non-marital father who registered before that date (or has not registered at all) is not a "parent" for adoption purposes. "Guardian" means "a person appointed by deed or will or by a court of competent jurisdiction to be the guardian of the child" (s.119(1)).

DISPENSING WITH PARENTAL AGREEMENT

While parental consent to adoption is central to respect for family integrity, there are circumstances where the parents are unable or wholly unsuited to fulfil any active role as such. Thus, there is provision for dispensing with parental consent to adoption. The Adoption Policy Review Group was critical of the prior law here and recommended a simple model for reform. In the event, the 2007 Act departs from the simple model and the consent of the child's parent or guardian may be dispensed with only where one of the following five grounds, some of which are similar to the previous tests and some of which are new, is satisfied (s.31(2) and (3)).

• *The parent or guardian is dead*

• *The parent of guardian cannot be found or is incapable of giving consent*

It will be very rare that the identity of a child's mother is not known but, occasionally, babies are abandoned and the mother is never traced. Before the court will conclude that a parent cannot be found, it will require evidence of the efforts made to locate the parent (*S v M* (1999)). Establishing that a parent is incapable of consenting to the adoption will normally require medical evidence of incapacity. Where parental incapacity is of a temporary nature, it is unlikely that a court would dispense with the parent's consent immediately.

• *The parent's or the guardian's continuing inability to satisfactorily discharge certain parental responsibilities or exercise certain parental rights*

This is the latest incarnation of a ground for dispensing with parental consent found in previous legislation. However, the wording differs in a number of significant respects and, thus, prior case law must be approached with the greatest of caution. Three elements must be present for this ground to be satisfied. First, the parent or guardian must have at least one of the parental responsibilities or parental rights other than simple contact (s.31(3)(c) and (4)). Second, the parent must be unable to discharge the responsibilities or to exercise the rights that he or she has satisfactorily (*Angus Council v C* (2000)). It is not clear whether the inability has to be in respect of all of the responsibilities or all of the rights. Previous legislation referred to the parent having "persistently failed" to fulfil the specified parental responsibilities. With the shift to the parent being "unable" to do so, the question arises, "What of a parent who is perfectly capable of doing what is required, but is simply not doing it?" The third requirement here is that the parent's inability to fulfil parental responsibilities or exercise parental rights is likely to continue.

- *The parent or guardian has lost parental responsibilities and parental rights by virtue of a permanence order (not granting authority for adoption) and is unlikely ever to regain them*

This provision is an innovation of the 2007 Act, as are permanence orders (discussed in Ch.6) themselves. First, it should be noted that this ground applies only to a permanence order containing the mandatory and ancillary provisions, but not a provision granting authority for the child to be adopted. Second, the parent or guardian must have lost all parental responsibilities and parental rights. If the parent or guardian has retained any such responsibility or right, this ground does not apply. Third, the court must determine that it is unlikely that the parent or guardian will regain any of the responsibilities or rights in the future.

- *That certain other provisions do not apply and the welfare of the child otherwise requires consent to be dispensed with*

This is a wholly new ground for dispensing with parental consent to adoption and one that is fraught with problems. The 2007 Act simply borrows from the equivalent legislation in England and Wales (Adoption and Children Act 2002 s.52(1)) and the warnings of the Adoption Policy Review Group, that the 2002 Act provision should be modified to make it human rights compliant, were ignored. In addition, the 2007 Act uses the term "welfare" in two distinct contexts. The first, under section 14, is this general obligation on the adoption agency and the court to consider the child's welfare throughout his or her life at all stages of the adoption process and a checklist of relevant factors is provided. The second is the present one, when the court is considering whether to dispense with parental consent. Is the welfare test in section 31 the same as that in section 14? It should be noted that this ground for dispensing with parental consent may only be used where the two previous grounds (inability to discharge parental responsibilities and parental rights or a permanence order being in place) do not apply.

Other situations where adoption may proceed

Aside from the opportunities for dispensing with parental consent outlined above, an adoption order may be made in the following circumstances:

- *A permanence order granting authority for the child to be adopted is in place*

As we shall see, a permanence order may (but need not) contain a provision granting authority for the child to be adopted. Where such a permanence order is in place, the adoption may proceed (s.31(7)).

- *Advance consent or placement under the Adoption and Children Act 2002*

Where each parent or guardian has given advance consent to adoption (and does not now oppose it) or the child has been placed by an adoption agency for adoption under the relevant statutory provision applying in England and Wales (2002 Act ss.19-21), an adoption order may be made in Scotland (2007 Act s.31(8) and (9)).

- *Adoption (Northern Ireland) Order 1987*

Where a child has been declared free for adoption under one of the relevant provisions applying in Northern Ireland (1987 Order, arts 17(1) or 18(1)), an adoption order may be made in Scotland (s.31(10)).

THE ADOPTISON PROCESS

Adoption services

Every local authority is obliged to provide adoption services designed to meet the needs of children who may be adopted; persons who have been adopted; their parents, guardians, siblings and grandparents; potential and actual adopters; and other persons affected by adoption (s.1(1)-(3)). The services that must be provided include arrangements for assessing children and prospective adopters and for placing children for adoption, providing information to any of the persons mentioned above and support services (s.1(4)). Adoption services must be registered under the Regulation of Care (Scotland) Act 2001.

Placement

Adoption is a serious matter and one which requires rigorous scrutiny. For that reason, adoptions cannot be arranged privately and anyone, other than an adoption service, who arranges an adoption is liable to prosecution, as is anyone who makes the placement or anyone who receives the child in such circumstances (s.75(1)). There are two exceptions to this rule. First, where the adopter is a relative of the child or part of a relevant couple as the partner of such a person, making the arrangements and placing the child need not be undertaken by an adoption service (s.75(2)). Secondly, a children's hearing may make it a condition of supervision that a child should live with people who are prospective adopters (Children (Scotland) Act 1995 s.70(3)). These exceptions aside, adoption arrangements must be made by an adoption service, being a local authority or a registered adoption service (s.119(1)).

A child may be placed for adoption only after all the options available for the child's future have been explored (s.14(2), (6) and (7)). The selection of suitable adopters requires consideration being given to the child's religious persuasion (assuming the child has one), racial origins and cultural and linguistic background (s.14(4)(c)). In addition, the agency must take account of any views the child has, the child's need for a stable family unit and the likely effect of the adoption on the child throughout his or her life, as well as the views of the child's parents, guardians and other relatives (s.14(4) and (5)). Thought should be given to whether there is a need to place the child in the same home as siblings and whether there should be continued contact with birth parents. Where the child is subject to a supervision requirement and an adoption service is satisfied that child should be placed for adoption, it must refer the child to the Principal Reporter (s.106).

Where the applicant or one of them is a parent, step-parent or relative of the child, or the child has been placed with the applicant by an adoption service, the adoption order may not be made until the child is 19 weeks old and unless the child has had a home with the applicants for the preceding 13 weeks (s.15(1)(a), (2) and (3)). In all other circumstances, no adoption order may be made unless the child has had a home with the applicants for the preceding 12 months and, thus, the child will be at least a year old (s.15(1)(b) and (4)).

Restrictions on removal of child pending adoption
Where a local authority has placed a child with a person with a view to adoption and the parents of the child have consented to the placement, it is an offence for any person to remove the child without the permission of the adoption service or the court (s.20). Where a person who has provided a home for a child for five years gives notice to the local authority of his or her intention to apply to adopt the child, it is an offence to remove the child from that person's care either prior to the making of the application for an adoption order or for a period of three months after the receipt by the local authority of the notification of intention, whichever occurs first (s.21). Where the child was looked after by the local authority prior to having a home with the applicant and remains looked after, the local authority can only remove the child in accordance with the procedure for return of a child placed for adoption or with the leave of a court or where removal is authorised by a children's hearing (s.23).

Application to court
The application for an adoption order is competent in either the Court of Session or the sheriff court, with most adoption orders being dealt with in the sheriff court, and the proceedings will be in private unless the court directs otherwise (s.28). A curator *ad litem* will be appointed to safeguard the child's interest and a reporting officer will be appointed to witness agreements to adoption (s.108(1)). The court grants or refuses the adoption and may make it subject to such conditions as it thinks fit (s.28(2) and (3)). Where the court refuses to grant the adoption order, it should consider whether the same applicants should be able to make a subsequent application in respect of the same child since, unless it indicates that such an application is competent, it will be incompetent unless a change of circumstances can be demonstrated to the later court (s.33). All adoptions are registered in the Adopted Children Register and an index thereof, along with a traceable link to the Register of Births, must now be maintained (ss.53-55). Access to the link between adoption and birth records is

restricted to adopted persons, those authorised by a court order and certain public bodies (s.55(3)).

THE EFFECTS OF ADOPTION

Since the 2007 Act only affects adoptions after it comes into force, it was necessary to leave Part IV of the Adoption (Scotland) Act 1978 in force in respect of adoptions that took place in the past. The consequences under each statute are much the same. An adoption order vests all parental responsibilities and parental rights in relation to the child in the adopters (s.28(2)) and, as a general rule, the child is no longer regarded as the child of his or her birth parents (s.40(4)). Where a child is adopted by a couple, he or she is treated by the legal system as the child of the couple (s.40(1) and (2)(a)). Where the adopter is a single person, the child is regarded as that person's child (s.40(1)). It will be remembered that, in the case of step-parent adoption, only the step-parent actually adopts the child and the partner-parent retains his or her original status. The effect is that the child is treated as the child of that couple (s.40(2)(b) and (3)). Thus, the general effect of adoption is to create a new family unit with all the attendant legal consequences. However, the following special effects and limitations on adoption should be noted.

- *Open adoption and adoption with contact*

The traditional view that adoption should terminate all contact between the child and the birth family has been challenged, not least because of the number of older children being adopted and the prevalence of step-parent adoptions. The term "open adoption" should be used with care, since it may mean many different practical arrangements in different circumstances. At a minimum, it may involve the exchange of information between the birth parents and the adopters in the early stage, with the exchange continuing, in some cases, but no direct contact between the birth parents and the child. However, it may involve direct contact between the child and his or her birth parents or other birth relatives and such an arrangement is known as "adoption with contact". When the court makes an adoption order it has long been able to attach "such terms and conditions as the court thinks fit" (s.28(3)) and, after some initial doubt (*A v B* (1987)), the courts accepted that this power could be used to provide for contact between a child and a birth parent or parents where this will be of some benefit to the child (*B v C* (1996)). It is now competent for a birth parent to seek post-adoption contact, but only with leave of the court (s.107 and Sched.2, para.9(2), amending the Children (Scotland) Act 1995 s.11). There is some ambiguity over the competency of a child seeking contact with a birth sibling, post-adoption (*D v H* (2004); *E v E* (2004)).

- *The prohibited degrees for purposes of marriage and civil partnership*

The adoption order does not terminate the relationship between the child and birth relatives for the purpose of the prohibited degrees of marriage or eligibility to register a civil partnership (s.41(1)(a)). In addition, marriage between an adopted child and an adoptive parent is prohibited and a parallel provision applies to civil partnerships (s.41(2)). Two children adopted into the same family, but otherwise unrelated, may marry.

- *Incest*

Adoption has no effect for the purpose of the law of incest, in so far as birth relatives are concerned, and sexual intercourse between the adoptive child and the adoptive parent is prohibited (s.41(1)(b)).

- *Pensions*

Adoption does not affect the entitlement to a pension that is in payment at the time of a person's adoption (s.42).

- *Insurance policies*

Where the birth parent has taken out an insurance policy with a friendly society, a collecting society or an industrial insurance company, the policy is not terminated by adoption but is transferred to the adoptive parents who acquire the rights and liabilities under the policy and they are treated as the persons who took out the policy (s.43).

- *Succession*

The modern position is that the adopted child takes a full place in his or her adoptive family for succession purposes, subject to the remaining exception that adoption has no effect on succession to titles, honours and coats of arms (Succession (Scotland) Act 1964 s.37(1)(a)).

- *Nationality and immigration*

A child who is a citizen of the UK and colonies retains that status even if adopted by persons who are not (s.41(3)). Where a foreign child is adopted by a UK citizen, the child normally acquires UK nationality (British Nationality Act 1981 s.1(5)). As we saw, provided that adoption proceedings began before the child's 18th birthday, the adoption order may be made after that landmark has been passed. However, the British Nationality Act 1981 has not been amended, so, in such cases, the adopted person does not acquire citizenship as a result of the adoption.

REVOKING AN ADOPTION ORDER

The 2007 Act continues the prior law by acknowledging two situations where an adoption order may be revoked. Since an adopted child may be adopted subsequently, the first adoption is superseded by the second. A "Convention adoption" (i.e. one under the Hague Convention on Adoption 1993, see below), may be annulled by the Court of Session on public policy grounds (s.68). These situations aside, an adoption order will only be declared to be null and revoked in cases of fundamental error (*J and J v C's Tutor* (1948) and *Cameron v McIntyre's Executor* (2006)).

INTER-COUNTRY AND FOREIGN ADOPTIONS

As a result of the small number of children available for adoption in Scotland and of sympathy for the plight of children who are suffering deprivation in other parts of the world, inter-country adoption has gained popularity. The Hague Convention on Jurisdiction, Applicable Law and Recognition of Decrees Relating to Adoptions sought to address international adoption as long ago as 1965, but that attempt met with very limited success and the United Kingdom was one of only three countries to ratify it. The second foray of the Hague Conference on Private International Law into the field, the Hague Convention on Protection of Children and Co-operation in Respect of Intercountry Adoption of 1993 (known as "the Hague Convention on Adoption"), has proved much more successful.

The Adoption (Intercountry Aspects) Act 1999 was passed to implement the provisions of the Hague Convention on Adoption throughout the UK and the Act came into force in Scotland on 1 June 2003. Since that date, there have been two kinds of adoptions having a foreign element and involving children coming to Scotland: convention adoptions and non-convention adoptions (including "overseas adoptions"). In addition, there will be cases of children going from Scotland to live abroad as part of the adoption process, although it is anticipated that these cases will be significantly fewer in number than those involving children coming here. The Hague Convention on Adoption 1993 applies to adoptions "which create a permanent parent-child relationship" where both "the state of origin" and "the receiving state" are parties to the Convention and much of the detail on how the system operates in the UK is provided for in regulations. Essentially, central authorities, already proven to be effective in the context of international child abduction, are used to administer intercountry adoptions.

Further reading:

E.E. Sutherland, *Child and Family Law*, 2nd edn (W. Green, 2008), Ch.5;
P.G.B. McNeill, *Adoption of Children in Scotland*, 3rd edn (W. Green 1998); 4th edn forthcoming 2009
Adoption Policy Review Group, *Report of Phase II: Adoption: Better Choices for Our Children*, (Scottish Executive, 2005), available at: *http://www.scotland.gov.uk/Publications/2005/06/27140607/06107* [accessed June 24, 2008]

---

5. PARENTAL RESPONSIBILITIES AND PARENTAL RIGHTS

Like other areas of law, the question of precisely what responsibilities parents owe to their children, and what rights they have in respect of them, developed over time. When the Scottish Law Commission turned its attention to these matters, it found that the law was in need of major reform (*Report on Family Law* (1992)). Part I of the Children (Scotland) Act 1995 is largely a product of its recommendations and the Act has been subject to amendment. References in this chapter are to the 1995 Act, as amended, unless otherwise stated.

PARENTAL RESPONSIBILITIES

The 1995 Act provides a clear statement of what responsibilities parents have towards their children. "*Parental* responsibilities" is just a convenient, short-hand term since, as we shall see, people other than the child's mother or father may acquire them. Parental responsibilities exist only so far as is practicable and in the interests of the child (s.1(1)). The child, or anyone acting on the child's behalf, has title to sue or defend in proceedings over parental responsibilities (s.1(3)). Parental responsibilities are:

• *To safeguard and promote the child's health, development and welfare* (s.1(1)(a)). This requires, not only that parents should protect the child's health, development and welfare, but that they should foster these interests actively. Clearly, a parent is required to meet the child's basic physical needs like housing, food and clothing. Providing for the child's health and welfare includes not only ensuring the child receives adequate medical care (*Finlayson (Applicant)* (1989); *McKechnie v McKechnie* (1990)), but that his or her psychological needs are met. While safeguarding and promoting the child's development has implications for formal education, it is directed at the development of the whole child.

• *To provide, in a manner appropriate to the stage of development of the child, (i) direction; and (ii) guidance* (s.1(1)(b)). The line between direction, connoting instructions, and guidance, suggesting a more advisory role, will not always be clear-cut. It should be remembered that the parental responsibility operates only where practicable, in the child's interests, alongside the child's rights to participate in decision-making and the rights of third parties, in certain contexts.

• *If the child is not living with the parent, to maintain personal relations and direct contact with the child on a regular basis* (s.1(1)(c)). The Act refers to "personal relations" as well as direct contact. This suggests communication on an emotional and psychological level, as well as simple presence. Essentially, a parent is required, at the very least, to keep in touch with a child, on a regular basis, where they are not living in the same household. Contact will often involve a great deal more, like attending the child's soccer matches, having the child to stay overnight or taking the child on holiday.

• *To act as the child's legal representative* (s.1(1)(d)). Essentially, there are three strands to this responsibility, but it is important to remember that children below the age of 16 have certain limited legal capacity of their own (Age of Legal Capacity (Scotland) Act 1991, discussed in Ch.3). First, the parental role involves administering any property belonging to the child (s.15(5)(a)). Where the child's parents, as legal representatives, administer property on the child's behalf, their actions are governed by the detailed provisions in sections 9 and 10 of the 1995

Act. The second strand to acting as the child's representative involves consenting to any transaction where the child is incapable of consenting on his or her own behalf (s.15(5)(b)). The third strand is the parental role in litigation. Essentially, the duty of a legal representative is to sue and defend in civil proceedings on behalf of a child who cannot do that for himself or herself, or where the child or young person does not wish to do so (s.15(6)).

In order to avoid any doubt about the lingering effect of common law responsibilities which may have existed in the past and the interaction of the 1995 Act with other statutes, the Act itself makes it clear that its provisions supersede the prior common law, but do not affect specific parental responsibilities set out in other statutes (s.1(4)). So, for example, the obligations in respect of aliment and child support are unaltered by the 1995 Act, as are obligations in respect of education. The responsibility to provide guidance ceases when the "child" is 18 (s.1(2)(b)), with all the other responsibilities terminating when the "child" reaches the age of 16 (s.1(2)(a)).

PARENTAL RIGHTS

Parental rights exist in order that parents can fulfil their parental responsibilities (s.2(1)) and they are subject to the same qualifications. Thus, they can only be exercised so far as is practicable and in the interests of the child. Again, *"parental* rights" is a short-hand term, since other people may be granted them by a court. Parental rights terminate when the child reaches the age of 16 (s.2(7)). Parental rights mirror parental responsibilities and they are the right:

• *To have the child living with him or her or otherwise to regulate the child's residence* (s.2(1)(a)). The right to determine a child's residence becomes relevant between family members when a dispute arises, usually because the parents separate or have never lived together, although other family members may ask the court to regulate residence, as may the child.

• *To control, direct or guide, in a manner appropriate to the stage of development of the child, the child's upbringing* (s.2(1)(b)). This is the corollary of the parental responsibility to provide direction and guidance to a child. However, it should be noted that the word "control" has been added, although it is doubtful that it adds anything to the content of the provision. Whereas the parental responsibility in respect of guidance lasts until the child is 18, the parental right to guide ends on the child's 16th birthday.

• *If the child is not living with the parent, to maintain personal relations and direct contact with the child on a regular basis* (s.2(1)(c)). This parental right is the mirror image of the parental responsibility to maintain personal relations and direct contact. Essentially, the parent is being given the right to do that which he or she is obliged to do.

• *To act as the child's legal representative* (s.2(1)(d)). Again, the parental right simply reflects the parental responsibility to act as the child's legal representative and is subject to the same qualifications.

The 1995 Act makes it clear that its provisions supersede the prior common law, but do not affect specific parental responsibilities set out in other statutes (s.2(5)). So, for example, parental rights in respect of a child's education remain.

WHO HAS PARENTAL RESPONSIBILITIES AND RIGHTS AUOMATICALLY?

Parental responsibilities and parental rights are acquired *automatically* by:
- *The child's mother* (s.3(1)(a)). All mothers acquire parental responsibilities and rights automatically from the moment of the child's birth.
- *The child's father, but only if he has been married to the mother at the time of the child's conception or subsequently* (s.3(1)(b)(i)). All "married fathers" (i.e. those married to their child's mother) are treated in the same way as are mothers, being endowed with automatic parental responsibilities and rights from the moment of the child's birth. In this context, "marriage" includes one which is voidable and one which is void but which both the parties believed in good faith to be valid at the time it was entered into (s.3(2)).
- *The child's non-marital father who registers as such* (s.3(1)(b)(ii)). Historically, non-marital fathers have been both tragic and demonised figures, "liable in the burdens of paternity without the privileges" (*Weepers v Heritors and Kirk-Session of Kennoway* (1844), *per* Lord Jeffrey at p.1173). Statute made gradual changes to their position and the Family Law (Scotland) Act 2006 amended the 1995 Act to enable them to acquire parental responsibilities and parental rights automatically, provided they registered (or re-registered) their paternity after the amendment came into force (4 May 2006). Registration requires the mother's consent, which failing, the father will have to seek a declarator of paternity (see Ch.4).

No other persons acquire parental responsibilities or rights *automatically*. However, this is no more than a starting point and the position may change subsequently. As we shall see, these parental responsibilities and parental rights may be restricted or removed by a court (s.11). A children's hearing may make a decision that has an enormous practical impact on the exercise of parental rights by, for example, requiring that the child should live somewhere other than with the parents (s.70). Where the child is adopted, the original parental responsibilities and rights come to an end and the adopters acquire them afresh (Adoption and Children (Scotland) Act 2007 ss.35 and 40). In addition, a host of persons may apply to the court for an order in relation to parental responsibilities and parental rights (s.11) and how the courts approach this issue will be considered presently. First, it is necessary to say a brief word about parental responsibilities and rights agreements.

Parental responsibilities and rights agreements
Prior to the 2006 Act amendment, non-marital fathers could not acquire parental responsibilities and parental rights automatically. The Scottish Law Commission had recommended the removal of all distinctions linked to parental marital status (*Report on Family Law* (1992) Rec.88), a position consistent with the U.N. Convention on the Rights of the Child

(arts 2 and 18). When it was enacting the Children (Scotland) Act 1995, Westminster chose to reject that recommendation and, instead, made a small concession by providing for a special form of agreement that the child's mother can make with the non-marital father, giving him full parental responsibilities and parental rights (s.4). Such agreements are only possible between the child's parents, irrespective of the age of the parents, and can only be made where the mother, herself, has full responsibilities and rights. The agreement must be in a form prescribed by the Scottish Ministers and registered in the Books of Council and Session. Such agreements, once registered, are stated to be "irrevocable" (s.4(4)), although, as is always the case with parental responsibilities and rights, the court retains its jurisdiction over the matter (s.11). There will now be little need for such agreements, but those registered in the past will remain relevant.

APPLICATIONS TO THE COURT IN RESPECT OF PARENTAL RESPONSIBILITIES AND PARENTAL RIGHTS

Only a fairly narrow range of people acquire parental responsibilities and parental rights automatically, yet many others, like step-parents, grandparents and other relatives, may be involved in a child's life in practical terms. The child's parents, these other interested parties and the child concerned may disagree over important matters in the child's life. Courts are not usually the best place to resolve disputes over the future arrangements for the care of children and the increase in the use of mediation and collaborative law, in finding a workable solution, is to be welcomed. However, some cases end up in court and the challenge for the legal system is to allow anyone with a legitimate concern about a child's future to bring the case before a court armed with adequate powers to deal with every situation.

Who may apply?

The following persons may apply to the court:

- *Any person who does not have and never has had parental responsibilities or parental rights in relation to the child but claims an interest* (s.11(3)(i)). This is the broadest and most far-reaching category of potential applicants and covers anyone who has never had parental responsibilities or parental rights in relation to the child. The applicant must "claim an interest"; that is, show some legitimate concern or connection with the child (*F v F* (1991)). Such applications will often be made by step-parents, grandparents or other relatives, but non-relatives may also use this provision. On any reasonable reading of it, the same-sex partner of a child's parent ought to be able to use this provision, but there is conflicting sheriff court authority on this point (*X v Y (Parental Rights: Insemination)* (2002), Glasgow Sheriff Court)); unreported decision of Sheriff McPartlin (2002, Edinburgh Sheriff Court). Similarly, there is conflicting sheriff court authority on whether a child may use this provision in, for example, seeking contact with a sibling (*D v H* (2004); *E v E* (2004)).
- *Any person who has parental responsibilities or rights* (s.11(3)(ii)). Where a person already has any of the parental responsibilities or parental

rights, he or she may apply to the court for regulation of them. Usually, the applicant is seeking to have someone else's parental responsibilities and rights regulated. Where, for example, married parents are divorcing, they will each have full parental responsibilities and rights. They need do nothing and each of them can continue with the same legal recognition of his or her status as a parent and agree the practical arrangements. If they cannot agree, either of them can go to the court and seek to remove or restrict the other's responsibilities and rights (*White v White* (2001)).

• *Any person who has had parental responsibilities or rights in relation to the child, but no longer has them and is not excluded by the Act* (s.11(3)(iii)). Various people may have had parental responsibilities or parental rights in the past but have lost them. Some of them, like a parent who has lost them on the application of the other parent, can still go back to the court in the future in an attempt to re-establish some aspect of their role as parent. However, an application for an order under s.11 may not usually be made by any person who had any parental responsibility or parental right but no longer has them because they have been extinguished by an adoption order or by an order under the Human Fertilisation and Embryology Act 1990 s.30(9) (s.11(3)(ab) and (4)). There is an exception here. Where a person has lost parental responsibilities or parental rights in one of these ways, he or she may still apply for a contact order, but only with leave of the court (s.11(3)(aa)).

• *The child* (s.11(5)). In the past, there was some doubt about whether or not a child could competently apply to the court for an order regulating parental rights being exercised over him or her. The 1995 Act puts the matter beyond doubt. As we have seen, there is debate over whether it is competent for a child to apply to the court in relation to parental responsibilities or parental rights in respect of another child.

The local authority has extensive powers in respect of children under Part II of the 1995 Act. For that reason, it is not permitted to apply under section 11 (s.11(5)). If a local authority is looking after a child, then a court may take account of its views when a section 11 order is being sought (*Mclean v Dornan* (2001)).

Action the court can take on its own initiative
Normally, the court will consider making an order because someone has made an application. However, the court can take the initiative in making an order. First, where no application has been made, or where the order sought by an applicant has been refused, the court may make an order nonetheless (s.11(3)(b)). Secondly, if it appears to the court that any of the grounds for referring a child to a children's hearing (see Ch.7) is satisfied in relation to a child, it may refer the matter to the Principal Reporter, who will consider whether it is necessary to refer the child to a hearing (s.54).

What can be applied for?
The 1995 Act provides that the court may make an order in relation to parental responsibilities, parental rights, guardianship or the administration of a child's property (s.11(1)). Often, the pursuer will be applying to be

given parental responsibilities or rights, but he or she may be seeking to have another person's rights removed or regulated. The court has very broad powers in granting any order it thinks fit (s.11(2)), provided the order does not contravene Council Regulation (EC) 2201/2003 (s.11(1A)). The orders most commonly applied for are residence orders and contact orders. Sometimes, a specific issue order may be sought to resolve a dispute over a particular matter such as the child's name or religious participation (*M v C* (2002)) or whether a parent may take a child to live abroad (*Shields v Shields* (2002)).

Court proceedings
Applications in relation to parental responsibilities and rights may be made alone or ancillary to another action in either the sheriff court or the Court of Session (s.11(1)). The onus of proof in applications in respect of parental responsibilities and rights lies on the applicant (*Sanderson v McManus* (1997); *White v White* (2001)). The standard of proof is on the balance of probabilities (*F v F* (1991)). The usual rules of evidence apply and hearsay evidence is admissible (Civil Evidence (Scotland) Act 1988 s.2).

Criteria for the court's decision
In reaching its decision, the court will apply the fundamental principles found in the 1995 Act (the "child lawyer's mantra"):
• *The welfare of the child is the paramount consideration* (s.11(7)(a)). There is no "welfare checklist", found in some other jurisdictions, since the Scottish Law Commission saw the danger of such a list being "necessary incomplete", encouraging a mechanistic approach and diverting attention from factors relevant to the particular case (*Report on Family Law* (1992)). However, the Family Law (Scotland) Act 2006 amended the 1995 Act to require the court to "have regard in particular" to two specific issues (s.11(7A)–(7E)). The first is the need to protect the child from abuse or the risk thereof, whether the abuse is directed at the child or at another person. The second applies to any order that would require two or more people to co-operate in its implementation, and the court is directed to consider whether it would be appropriate to make the order. In addition, the European Court has sent a clear message that decisions should be based on assessing the impact of specific factors on the particular child, rather than generalised assumptions (*Palau-Martinez v France* (2005)).

These matters aside, a host of factors are relevant to what will serve, or detract from, a child's welfare and each case will depend on its own facts and circumstances. Courts in the past have considered such matters as physical welfare (*Clayton v Clayton* (1995)), emotional welfare (*Geddes v Geddes* (1987); *Treasure v McGrath* (2006)), the importance of the status quo and established relationships (*McG v McG* (2006)), educational welfare (*Clayton v Clayton* (1995)), the impact of religion (*McKechnie v McKechnie* (1990)), and parental lifestyle (*Casey v Casey* (1989); *Brixey v Lynas* (1994); *Pearson v Pearson* (1999)).
• *The child must be given the opportunity to express his or her views and account will be taken of these views in the light of the child's age and*

maturity (s.11(7)(b)). The court has stressed the importance of this principle repeatedly (*Shields v Shields* (2002)) and it may have considerable impact on the outcome of a case (*Treasure v McGrath* (2006)), albeit the child's age and maturity will be kept in mind (*Casey v Casey* (1989)).

• *The court will not make any order unless to do so will be better than making no order at all* (s.11(7)(a)). It may be that in a particular case, no order is necessary or no purpose would be served by making one (*Treasure v McGrath* (2006)). In addition, a lack of parental co-operation may suggest no order should be made (s.11(7D); *Russell v Russell* (1991)), but not every court will permit the unco-operative parent to determine the outcome of the case (*Davidson v Smith* (1998)).

Interaction of court and other orders
There has long been scope for the exercise of courts' "private law" powers to clash with their "public law" powers or the decision of a children's hearing, so it important to be clear about which takes precedence. Once a permanence order (see Ch.6) is in place, a court may not make an order under section 11, except where that order relates to the granting of interdict or the appointment of a judicial factor (s.11A). Where a section 11 order is already in place when a permanence order is granted, the permanence order revokes the section 11 order (Adoption and Children (Scotland) Act 2007 s.88). A supervision requirement from a children's hearing (see Ch.7) takes precedence, in terms of regulating residence or contact, over a section 11 order (*Aitken v Aitken* (1978)). However, the fact that a supervision requirement is in place does not preclude a person from applying for a residence or contact order (*P v P* (2000)).

FULFILLING PARENTAL RESPONSIBILITIES AND EXERCISING PARENTAL RIGHTS
Where more than one person has responsibilities and rights in respect of a child, the general rule is that each of the persons may exercise the right alone without the consent of the other (s.2(2)). However, the freedom to exercise parental rights alone does not entitle a person to remove a child from the United Kingdom without appropriate consent (s.2(3)). The fundamental principles apply to fulfilling parental responsibilities and exercising parental rights and the Act makes special provision requiring any person who is taking a major decision in this context to give the child the opportunity to express his or her views and to take these views into account in the light of the child's age and maturity (s.6). While a person who has responsibilities or rights may not surrender or transfer any part of them, the holder is permitted to arrange for them to be met or exercised by another person acting on the holder's behalf (s.3(5)). No arrangement of this sort affects a person's liability for failure to meet parental responsibilities, so the byword is "delegation, but not abdication" (s.3(6)). The power to delegate covers a very wide range of possible situations and would include a parent who uses an occasional babysitter, a full-time nanny, or day care.

CHILD ABDUCTION

As we have seen, the legal system provides extensive machinery to regulate where a child may live and with whom. Despite that, a parent may be dissatisfied with the arrangements and may take the law into his or her own hands, either by taking the child away, in breach of an agreement or a court order, or by refusing to return the child after an authorised visit. Illegal removal of a child from a person entitled to control the child's residence is governed by both criminal and civil law, as is wrongful retention of the child. At common law, the crime of *plagium* is the stealing of a child from his or her parents. It was long believed that it could be committed by a parent who has no right to determine the child's residence (*Downie v H.M. Advocate* (1984)), although that proposition was thrown into doubt by one sheriff court decision (*Orr v K* (2003)). It is an offence for a "person connected with a child" to remove the child from Scotland without the consent of the child's parents, guardians and any person named by a court as the person with whom the child should live (Child Abduction Act 1984).

However, it is the array of civil law provisions that are of greater importance, in practical terms, in securing the return of a child. Within the United Kingdom, special provisions have ensured the quick return of children taken from one jurisdiction to another (Family Law Act 1996), although these must now be read along with the relevant European Union regulations governing recognition and enforcement of rights of custody and access (still the terms used in international instruments) and a host of other matters, including child abduction within the EU (Council Regulation (EC) 2201/2003, known as "Brussels II *bis*"). Beyond Europe and depending on the country where the child is located, the Hague Convention on the Civil Aspects of International Child Abduction (1980) and the Hague Convention on Jurisdiction, Applicable Law, Recognition, Enforcement and Co-operation in respect of Parental Responsibility and Measures for the Protection of Children (1996) may apply. Broadly, these Conventions create mutual obligations between contracting states to effect the speedy return of children to the appropriate country. Where a child has been abducted from Scotland to a Convention country, the parent in Scotland can make use of the provisions. Conversely, the law provides for a child who has been brought to Scotland illegally being returned to his or her place of habitual residence. Where a child has been abducted to a country which is not a party to the Conventions, the party seeking to secure the child's return will have to rely on the domestic law of that country and, sometimes, the prospects of the child's return are not good.

FINANCIAL SUPPORT FOR CHILDREN

Scots law has always recognised that parents are obliged to support their children. Only when they are unable to do so does the obligation fall on the state. The traditional mechanism, the law on aliment, which is administered by the courts, is now found in the Family Law (Scotland) Act 1985. In 1991, a separate system for dealing with financial support for most children was introduced by the Child Support Act 1991. While the intention was that child support would replace aliment for children in many cases, the latter remains relevant. Each is discussed below.

Child support
The child support system as originally introduced and administered was widely acknowledged to be something of a disaster and various attempts have been made to salvage it by amending the 1991 Act (Child Support Act 1995; Child Support, Pensions and Social Security Act 2000). The most recent – and most radical – attempt is found in the Child Maintenance and Other Payments Act 2008. Since the changes in the 2008 Act will be implemented over a number of years, it is necessary to outline the current system and that which will replace it.

The parties
Child support applies only where the following parties are present:
- A "qualifying child". Broadly, this means a child under the age of 16, but unmarried children can be covered up to the age of 18 if the parent is still claiming state benefit in respect of them, or 19 if the child is still at school (s.55). For there to be a "qualifying child", one or both of the parents must be a "non-resident parent" (s.3(1)).
- A "non-resident parent" (formerly, "absent parent"). Such a parent is one who is not living in the same household as the child (s.3(2)). "Parent" covers only mothers and fathers and does not include step-parents (s.54).
- A "person with care". This is the person with whom the child has a home or who usually provides the day-to-day care for the child (s.3(3)) and will often be one of the child's parents (known as the "parent with care").

The present system
The child support system is currently administered by the Child Support Agency (CSA), a UK-wide agency based at Falkirk. Essentially, it applies to two categories of people, those who must use it and those who may choose to do so. Where a parent with care is in receipt of a broad range of state benefits, including income support and family credit, he or she must authorise the Secretary of State to take action to recover child support maintenance from the non-resident parent (s.6(1)). Where a person is required to give such authorisation, he or she is obliged to co-operate in seeking a maintenance calculation and in providing the necessary information and, in particular, information enabling the non-resident parent to be traced (s.6(5)–(9)). Such authorisation is not required where co-operation in seeking a maintenance calculation would expose the mother or any child living with her to the risk of "harm or undue distress" (s.6(8)). That exception aside, failure to co-operate may result in the parent's benefits may be cut by up to 40 per cent for up to three years, with possible extensions of this period for as long as she refuses to disclose the father's identity (s.46).

In addition to those who must use the child support system, it is available to many others. Anyone who qualifies as a person with care, whether a parent or not, may apply for a maintenance calculation under the Act, as can the non-resident parent (s.4(1)). Any child aged 12 or over and habitually resident in Scotland may apply for a maintenance calculation (s.7(1)). Applications for a maintenance calculation cannot be made where there is already one in force (s.4(9)).

The calculation of child support is based wholly on the non-resident parent's net weekly income, subject to a current cap of £2,000 *per* week. In order to accommodate the range of possible payers, four rates apply. They are:

- The nil rate, i.e. paying nothing – applying to persons of a "prescribed description" (e.g. parents under 18 years old, prisoners) whose net weekly income is less than £5 *per* week;
- The flat rate – currently £5 *per* week – applying to a person whose net weekly income is less than £100 *per* week, or who receives certain prescribed benefits, or whose partner receives certain prescribed benefits;
- The reduced rate – calculated according to a formula – applying to persons whose net weekly income is between £100 and £200;
- The basic rate – the notional norm, being the following percentage of net weekly income: 15 per cent for one qualifying child, 20 per cent for two qualifying children and 25 per cent for three or more qualifying children (Sch.1).

There is provision for special cases (e.g. a child who is in hospital), variations (to accommodate a special circumstance like tax liability) and revisions. Appeal lies to a Child Support Appeal Tribunal, then to a Child Support Commissioner, and then, on a question of law and with permission, to the Court of Session (ss.20-25). Once a maintenance calculation has been made, the CSA has various means by which to enforce payment, including deductions from earnings orders; liability orders, enforceable by diligence; disqualifying the non-payer from driving and imprisonment (ss.30-40). A parent may not use the courts to enforce child support even if the CSA fails to do so *(Kehoe v Secretary of State for Work and Pensions* (2006)).

Child support and the courts
The main thrust of the 1991 Act is to exclude the courts from determining issues of financial support for children. Where a child support officer "would have jurisdiction to make a maintenance calculation . . . no court shall exercise any power which it would otherwise have to make, vary or revive any maintenance order" (s.8). There are a host of exceptions to this general rule. Many of them are set out explicitly in the 1991 Act, others implicit in it. The most important arise in respect of "top up" awards, where a parent is particularly wealthy (s.8(6)); additional payments to cover educational expenses, like school fees (s.8(7)); and expenses attributable to a child's disability (s.8(8) and (9)). In addition, child support is inapplicable where one of the parties is habitually resident abroad (s.44).

The new system

The Child Maintenance and Other Payments Act 2008 effects the most radical overhaul of the child support system to date. It abolishes the CSA and replaces it with the Child Maintenance and Enforcement Commission (C-MEC), which will take over CSA responsibilities and administer the new system (ss.1–14). The emphasis in the 2008 Act is on allowing all parents to make their own arrangements for child maintenance and benefits recipients will no longer be compelled to use the child support system. The "reduced benefits direction", used against the parent with care who would not co-operate in helping to track down the non-resident parent, will be abolished and a greater part of amounts paid in child support will be disregarded when calculating a wider range of benefits (s.15).

Essentially, there will be two routes to an effective child support arrangement:

- Independent agreement between the parents (whether recorded in a court order or the Books of Council and Session or not (s.35))
- Using C-MEC

There is an incentive for parents to reach agreement since C-MEC will have the power to charge for its services (s.6). Parents already in the system will be able to choose between staying with C-MEC or going it alone.

The calculation of child support will change slightly. While the non-resident parent's income will continue to be the sole basis for calculation, in future, the *gross* (not net) weekly income will be relevant, with the "ceiling" above which income is disregarded being raised from £2,000 to £3,000. The existing "nil rate" will continue to apply and the "flat rate" will increase from £5 to £7. These cases aside, the basic rate of child maintenance will be calculated on the following percentage of gross income between £200 and £800 per week:

- 12 per cent for one qualifying child;
- 16 per cent for two qualifying children;
- 19 per cent for three or more qualifying children.

For non-resident parents earning over £800 per week, an additional amount will be payable, based on the income between £800 and £3,000 as follows:

- 9 per cent for one qualifying child;
- 12 per cent for two qualifying children;
- 15 per cent for three or more qualifying children (s.16 and Sch.4).

C-MEC will retain all the sanctions for non-payment currently available to the CSA, but the making of a liability order will become an administrative decision and will no longer require an order from the sheriff, albeit there will be a right to appeal to an appeal tribunal against C-MEC's decision. New sanctions will include extending the use of deduction orders to current and deposit accounts, lump sum deduction orders, passport confiscation and subjecting the non-payer to a curfew, backed up by electronic tagging (ss.20–30).

Aliment

Aliment remains relevant where the child support legislation does not apply and is of particular significance where the obligation to support a child falls on a non-parent, like a step-parent or other relative. Aliment may be claimed by a person up to the age of 24, who is still in full-time education or training, and is of particular importance to students (*Park v Park* (2000)). The Family Law (Scotland) Act 1985 is the relevant statute here.

For the purpose of aliment, a "child" is a person:

- Under 18 years old, or,
- Under 25 years old, "who is reasonably and appropriately undergoing instruction at an educational establishment, or training for employment or for a trade, profession or vocation" (s.1(5)).

Such a child is owed an obligation of aliment by:

- His or her mother (s.1(1)(c));
- His or her father (s.1(1)(c));
- Any person who has "accepted" the child into his or her family (s.1(1)(d)). "Acceptance" denotes more than simply living under the same roof as the child, and can render other family members, like an aunt or uncle (*Inglis v Inglis* (1987)) or a step-parent, liable for aliment. A person is not regarded as accepting a child where the child has been boarded out to that person by a local or public authority or a voluntary organisation.
- The executor of a deceased person or any person who has been enriched by succession to the estate of a deceased person owing the obligation (s.1(4)).

Where more than one person owes an obligation to aliment a child, there is no automatic order of liability, although when aliment is being sought from one person, the obligations of other persons will be taken into account (s.4(2)).

How much?

The obligation of aliment is to provide "such support as is reasonable in the circumstances" (s.1(2)), having regard to:

- The needs and resources of parties (s.4(1)(a)). The present and foreseeable needs and resources of both the pursuer and defender are relevant here. For example, where a school pupil had a part-time job, her father was able to argue that the amount of aliment payable by him should be reduced (*Wilson v Wilson* (1987)). In assessing the parties' respective needs and resources, the court will look at actual income, expenditure in respect of appropriate items and at evidence of an individual's lifestyle, including such matters as foreign holidays (*Joshi v Joshi* (1998)).
- The earning capacities of parties (s.4(1)(b)). It should be noted that it is not simply the *actual* earnings of the parties which are relevant, but their earning *capacities*. Where a person has a well-paid job and gives it up when confronted with a claim for aliment, what he or she was

earning will usually be taken into account, as a reflection of earning capacity.
- All the circumstances of the case (s.4(1)(c)). This consideration acknowledges that every case will turn on its own facts. However, amongst other relevant circumstances mentioned in the Act is the fact that the defender is supporting another person, whether or not he or she is under an obligation to do so (s.4(3)(a)).

A person's conduct is irrelevant unless it would be "manifestly inequitable" to ignore it (s.4(3)(b)).

Defences
The fact that a child is living with the defender is no bar to raising an action for aliment (s.2(6)). However, it is open to the defender to demonstrate that he or she is fulfilling the alimentary obligation by supporting the child in his or her own home and will continue to do so (s.2(7)). In addition, where the child is at least 16 years old, it is open to the defender to make an offer to maintain the child in his or her own household. However, such an offer only constitutes a good defence where it would be reasonable to expect the child to accept the offer (s.2(8)). In assessing "reasonableness", the court is directed to have regard to "any conduct, decree or other circumstances" (s.2(9)). An offer of this kind is no defence where the child is below the age of 16 (s.2(8)).

How does aliment work?
An action for aliment may be raised in either the Court of Session or the sheriff court (s.2(1)), and may be brought by way of an independent action or in the course of other proceedings (s.2(2)). The action may be raised by the child or, on behalf of a child under 18, by a parent, a guardian, or a person with whom the child lives or who is seeking a residence order (s.2(3)). A woman may raise an action on behalf of her unborn child, but the action will not be heard and disposed of until after the birth (s.2(5)).

The court may grant decree in an action for aliment and, in so doing, may make two kinds of awards. The first, and most common, is to order the making of periodical payments for a definite or indefinite period or until a specific event happens (s.3(1)(a)). Secondly, it may also order the making of an alimentary payment of an occasional or special nature to cover expenses like a school trip (s.3(1)(b)). Such awards should not be used as a means of substituting a lump sum for periodical payments (s.3(2)). In granting decree, the court can backdate an award (s.3(1)(c)) and a smaller sum than that sought may be awarded (s.3(1)(d)).

Either the pursuer or the defender may request variation or recall of an order for aliment on showing that there has been a material change of circumstances (s.5(1)). What is, or is not, a material change of circumstances will turn on the individual facts of each case and the only such circumstance spelt out in the Act is the making of a child maintenance calculation under the Child Support Act 1991 (s.5(1A)). The court has the power to backdate any variation (s.5(2)) and order repayment of sums paid under the original decree. In the course of considering variation or recall, it may make an interim award (s.5(3)).

Further reading:
E.E. Sutherland, *Child and Family Law*, 2nd edn (W. Green, 2008), Chs 6–8.

---

6. CHILD PROTECTION

The legal system takes a number of different approaches to child protection. It defines who has responsibilities for children, what they are, and adjudicates in cases of dispute (see Ch.5). It seeks to deny children access to particular commodities or dangers (see Ch.3). In this chapter, we will consider the role of the state through the duties placed on the local authority, the court orders it may seek and other civil and criminal processes in place designed to protect children (and others) from specific individuals. While the state plays a crucial role in seeking to protect children from harm, it must remain vigilant to ensure that it complies with human rights standards when it intervenes in the family. In this, articles 6 (right to a fair trial), 8 (right to respect for private and family life) and 14 (prohibition of discrimination) of the European Convention on Human Rights may be of particular relevance (*Authority Reporter, Edinburgh v U* (2008)).

Scots law had long sought to protect children from abuse and neglect and, as in many other jurisdictions, domestic law reform has often been prompted by examples of the system failing specific children. While the then-current system was already under review, there is no doubt that the infamous *"Orkney Case"* (*Sloan v B* (1991)) and the recommendations of the inquiry that followed (*Report into the Inquiry into the Removal of Children from Orkney in 1991* (1992)) were instrumental in shaping the current law and practice. The primary legislation is Part II of the Children (Scotland) Act 1995 and references below are to that statute, as amended, unless otherwise stated. Despite progress made by the 1995 Act, numerous examples illustrate continuing failures in the child protection system. Individual children have died at the hands of family members and others have been subjected to systematic and long-term abuse despite their cases being known to the authorities. Cases of abuse in state-sanctioned institutions, both many years ago and more recently, have emerged. Yet another review of the system, under the umbrella title *Getting It Right for Every Child* (known as "GIRFEC") led to consultation on the Draft Children's Services (Scotland) Bill (2005). That process revealed both strengths and weaknesses in the proposed legislation and the current Scottish Government is taking its own version of the project forward.

LOCAL AUTHORITY OBLIGATIONS TO CHILDREN

The starting point is that children should normally be cared for within their own families (s.22(1)(b)) and it is only where the child's welfare cannot be served adequately in that setting that removal becomes an option. While the 1995 Act places much of the responsibility for child protection on the local authority, which it fulfils largely through its social work department, it should be remembered that others, like educators, health care professionals, the police and voluntary organisations, all play crucial roles. That the local authority should approach its obligations to children in a co-ordinated manner is demonstrated by the fact that it is required to prepare, publish, and keep under review a plan of the provision of services to children in its area (s.19).

The local authority often has particular duties towards "children in need". This is a term with a special statutory meaning and a "child in need" is one:

- Who is unlikely to achieve or maintain a reasonable standard of health or development unless services are provided for him or her by the local authority; or
- Whose health or development is likely to be impaired significantly unless such services are provided; or
- Who is disabled; or
- Who is affected adversely by the disability of another member of his or her family (s.93(4)(a)).

The local authority is *obliged* to safeguard and promote a child in need's welfare by providing services for the child directly and providing services for another member of the child's family or for the family as a whole, if such provision is designed to safeguard or promote the child's welfare (s.22(1)(a)).

Day care for pre-school and other children

In respect of children in need, each local authority *shall* provide day care for children under five years old (s.27(1)) and after school care (s.27(3)) "as is appropriate" but, it appears, it has considerable discretion (*Crossan v South Lanarkshire Council* (2006)) . While it may provide such care for other children, it is not obliged to do so. The Scottish Commission for the Regulation of Care Services now regulates and oversees private childminding and day care (Regulation of Care (Scotland) Act 2001).

Children with disabilities and those affected by the disability of another person

A child may have a disability and require special assistance or facilities, or may be affected by the disability of another family member, like a parent or a sibling. Such a child falls within the definition of a child in need. The local authority must provide assistance to such children in order "to minimise the adverse effect" of the disability on them and to give them "the opportunity to lead lives which are as normal as possible" but, again, it has considerable discretion in how it does so (s.23(1)). If called upon to do so by the child's parent or guardian, the local authority must carry out an assessment of the child's needs or the carer's ability to provide care (s.23(3)).

Provision of accommodation for children
The local authority is obliged to provide accommodation for a child below the age of 18 where he or she appears to require it because:
- No one has parental responsibilities for the child;
- The child is lost or abandoned; or
- The child's carer is prevented, whether or not permanently and for whatever reason, from providing suitable accommodation or care (s.25(1)).

In addition, the local authority may provide a child with accommodation if it considers that to do so would safeguard or promote the child's welfare (s.25(2)). Accommodation may be provided for 18 to 21-year-olds in similar circumstances (s.25(3)).

One way in which the local authority may discharge its obligation to provide accommodation is by placing the child with a relative and "kinship care" is receiving increasing attention in Scotland. Another way is through the use of foster care. Organisation of foster care is the responsibility of the local authority and the Fostering of Children (Scotland) Regulations 1996 govern the operation of fostering. It should be remembered that a child living with foster carers is still being "looked after" by the local authority and its obligations to the child continue.

Obligations to children being looked after by the local authority
The local authority must safeguard and promote the welfare of every child it is looking after and the child's welfare must be its paramount concern (s.17(1)(a)). It must provide advice and assistance to prepare the child for a time when the local authority is no longer looking after him or her (s.17(2)). In so far as it is consistent with the child's welfare, the local authority must promote personal relations and direct contact on a regular basis between the child and any person with parental responsibilities in relation to the child (s.17(1)(c)). It must take reasonable steps to ascertain the child's views before making any decision with respect to the child and take those views into account in the light of the child's age and maturity (ss.17(3)(a) and 17(4)(a)). In addition, the local authority is obliged to ascertain the views of the child's parents, non-parents who have parental rights in respect of the child and any other person the local authority considers relevant, and to take any views expressed by these persons into account (ss.17(3)(b)–(d) and 17(4)(b)). In fulfilling its obligations to the child, the local authority is permitted to act in a manner inconsistent with its duties under section 17 where such action is necessary to protect members of the public from serious harm (s.17(5)).

After-care for young people leaving care

Where a young person was being looked after by the local authority at the time he or she ceased to be of school age or at any time thereafter, the local authority is obliged to advise, guide and assist that young person until he or she reaches 19, unless the local authority is satisfied that the young person's welfare does not require it (s.29(1)). In addition, the young person may request such advice, guidance and assistance until he or she is 21 and the local authority may provide it (s.29(2)). Again, the local authority is obliged to carry out an assessment of the young person's needs if called upon to do so (s.29(5)).

Financial assistance towards expenses of education or training

Where a young person has been looked after by the local authority at the time he or she ceased to be of school age or at any time thereafter, the local authority may make a grant to the young person to meet expenses connected with education or training or contribute towards accommodation or maintenance of such a young person while he or she is under 21 (s.30(1) and (2)). Where a local authority has provided this form of assistance prior to the young person reaching the age of 21, it may continue to provide it thereafter (s.30(3)).

COURT ORDERS

Often the local authority can provide a given family with support and, thus, enable a child to remain at home. However, the local authority may continue to harbour doubts about the home environment. In other cases, the local authority may be convinced that a child is at risk in the family home. There are a number of court orders that can be sought in these circumstances. Before we discuss them, it is necessary to examine the application of the fundamental principles of child law to such situations and what is meant by "relevant persons", the other key people in this context.

Fundamental principles

The fundamental principles which we have seen operating in the family setting also apply in the context of child protection. When a court or a children's hearing is reaching a decision, it must usually consider these principles. However, they do not apply to all such decisions and may be subject to qualification, as set out below.

- *The welfare of that child throughout his or her childhood shall be the paramount consideration* (s.16(1)). The welfare principle applies throughout Part II of the 1995 Act, and it is welfare throughout the child's childhood, until the child reaches the age of 18, that is relevant. Deviation from this principle is permitted, for example, "for the purpose of protecting members of the public from serious harm" (s.16(5)).
- *The child must be given the opportunity to express his or her views in certain circumstances and regard must be had to these views in the light of the child's age and maturity* (s.16(2) and (4)). As we shall see in Ch.7, the child's participation has always been central to the children's

hearings system. In the context of courts, children must usually be given the opportunity to participate when decisions are being taken about them. However, while the child's views are relevant to most decisions under this part of the Act, they need not be considered in all cases. For example, a sheriff need not consider them when deciding whether to grant a child protection order.

- *No order should be made unless making the order would be better than making no order at all* (s.16(3)). Presumed non-intervention applies to most decisions under Part II of the Act where a child's views are relevant. Where presumed non-intervention applies, it determines whether an order should or should not be granted. Once an order has been granted, the appropriate level of intervention is not subject to any presumption of minimal intervention.

Relevant persons

Before we look at the orders a court can make, it is important to be clear about what is meant by "relevant persons". This term was coined by the 1995 Act to indicate that people other than parents might be important in a child's life and to make those people part of the decision-making process. Relevant persons are:

- Any parent enjoying parental responsibilities or parental rights under the 1995 Act;
- Any person in whom parental responsibilities or parental rights are vested by virtue of the 1995 Act;
- Any person in whom parental responsibilities or parental rights are vested by, under or by virtue of a permanence order; and
- Any person who has or appears to have charge of or control over a child, otherwise than in the course of employment (s.93(2)(b); see also, *Children's Reporter v D* (2008) and *SS v Children's Reporter* (2008)).

Child Assessment Orders

A child assessment order (CAO) provides for the opportunity to determine whether the local authority's suspicion of abuse or neglect is justified, where such assessment would not be possible without the court giving its authority, and may involve removing the child from the home (s.55). Only a local authority may apply for a CAO and, before exercising his or her discretion to grant an order, the sheriff must be satisfied that:

- The local authority has reasonable grounds to suspect that the child is being so treated (or neglected) that he or she is suffering, or is likely to suffer, significant harm; and
- Such assessment is necessary to establish whether the child is being so treated (or neglected); and
- Such assessment is unlikely to be carried out, or be carried out satisfactorily, unless the order is granted (s.55).

A CAO may be appropriate, for example, to authorise medical examination of the child in the face of parental opposition. It should be noted that the 1995 Act specifically preserves the child's right to consent to medical examination (s.90). Thus, a CAO cannot be used to override the opposition of a child who understands what is involved. A CAO cannot last for more than seven days and it must specify when assessment is to begin (s.55(3)). It may deal with other matters like where the child is to reside during assessment and who may have contact with the child (s.55(4) and (5)). Where a CAO results in the child's removal from home, he or she becomes a child being looked after by the local authority and the local authority acquires the responsibility for safeguarding his or her welfare (s.17(1) and (6)(c)). Where an application is made for a CAO and the sheriff finds that the more stringent grounds justifying the granting of a child protection order are satisfied, the Act provides that he or she "shall" make the latter (s.55(2)).

Having assessed the child, the local authority may conclude that its suspicions were unfounded and that no further action is required, or that there is some cause for concern, but that voluntary arrangements can be made with the family to address the concern. However, the local authority may conclude that the case should be referred to the Principal Reporter (see Ch.7) or that it should apply for an exclusion order or a child protection order.

Exclusion Orders

The 1995 Act introduced a new kind of exclusion order (EO), modelled on that available under the Matrimonial Homes (Family Protection) (Scotland) Act 1981 (see Ch.9), to provide for the removal of the alleged abuser from the family home (ss.76–80). Previously, where there was concern over a child's safety, it was usually the child who was removed, and it was likely that at least some children saw their removal as implying that the problem was somehow their fault. Only a local authority may apply for an EO and a sheriff may exclude a named person from a child's family home if he or she is satisfied that:

- The child has suffered, is suffering, or is likely to suffer, significant harm as a result of any conduct, or threatened or reasonably apprehended conduct, of the named person; and
- The making of the order (i) is necessary to protect the child, irrespective of whether the child is residing in the family home at the moment, and (ii) would better safeguard the child's welfare than removal of the child from the family home; and
- If the order is made, there will be someone specified in the application (an "appropriate person") who is capable of looking after the child and any other family member who lives in the household and requires care and who is, or will be, residing in the family home (s.76(2)).

However, an EO must be refused if to grant it would be "unjustifiable or unreasonable" (s.76(9)–(11)). In assessing this criterion, the sheriff must consider all the circumstances of the case, including:

- The conduct of the members of the child's family;
- The respective needs and financial resources of the members of that family;

- The extent to which the home is used in connection with a trade, business or profession; and
- Any requirement that the named person should reside in the family home, like the fact that it is let or occupied by an employee as an incident of employment.

He or she must then weigh these considerations in the light of the fundamental principles (s.16; *Russell v W* (1998)).

The named person and certain other people, like a landlord, have a right to be heard or represented before a final decision on the application for an EO is made (s.76(3)). In the meantime, the sheriff may grant an interim EO (s.76(4) and (6)). Where an EO is sought and the sheriff is satisfied that the conditions justifying a child protection order are met, he or she may grant a child protection order (s.76(8)). The effect of an EO is to suspend the named person's right of occupancy in the home to which the order relates and prevent him or her from entering that home except with the permission of the local authority that applied for the order (s.77(1)). Various ancillary orders may be attached to an EO, like an interdict prohibiting the named person from removing relevant items from the home or prohibiting the named person from entering or remaining in a specified area within the vicinity of the home (s.77(3)). At any time when an EO is in force, the local authority may apply to the sheriff for a power of arrest to be attached to it (s.78). An EO under the 1995 Act lasts for no longer than six months and may last for a shorter period of time where that is specified in the order itself (s.79(1) and (2)). However, when an EO is due to expire, there is nothing to prevent the local authority applying for another.

Child Protection Orders (CPOs)

CPOs were introduced by the 1995 Act to replace the older mechanism, the place of safety order, which had been the subject of much criticism. CPOs are intended to be more flexible and there are detailed provisions on their implementation, duration, review, recall and variation. Application for a CPO may be made to a sheriff in two distinct sets of circumstances and the granting of a CPO is discretionary.

First, any person (including the child or a relative) may apply for a CPO on the basis that:

- The child is being so treated (or neglected) that he or she is suffering significant harm or that he or she will suffer such harm if not removed and kept in a place of safety or if he or she does not remain in the place where he or she is being accommodated; and
- The order is necessary to protect the child from such harm (or further harm) (s.57(1)).

Secondly, a local authority may apply for a CPO on the basis that:

- The child is being so treated (or neglected) that he or she is suffering, or will suffer, significant harm, and
- It is making enquiries to allow it to decide whether it should take any action to safeguard the welfare of the child, and

- Its enquiries are being frustrated by access to the child being unreasonably denied, such access being required as a matter of urgency (s.57(2)).

In reaching his or her decision, the sheriff must regard the child's welfare as the paramount consideration (s.16(1)). There is no requirement to take the child's views into account, although how the child feels about the possibility of being removed from home or detained elsewhere will be relevant in considering whether the order will serve the child's welfare. In addition, the local authority should have tried to ascertain the child's views (s.17(3)). The sheriff must make an immediate decision on an application for a CPO (Act of Sederunt (Child Care and Maintenance Rules) 1997 r.3.31). There is no appeal against the sheriff's decision to grant or refuse a CPO (s.51(15)). In addition to authorising the removal and retention of a child, a CPO may provide that a child should not be removed from a specified place, require a person to produce the child, and provide that the location of the child's whereabouts should not be disclosed to particular persons (s.57(4)). Similarly, the sheriff may make a direction on contact between the child and any other persons, like the child's parents (s.58(1)).

Once granted, a CPO ceases to have effect if no attempt to implement it has been made within 24 hours (s.60(1)). Where a CPO has resulted in a child being taken to a place of safety or kept in such a place, it must be subject to review on the second working day after implementation (s.60(2)). Review may be by means of an application to the sheriff (s.60) or to a children's hearing (s.59). In the latter case, there is the possibility of a second review, within two working days of the first children's hearings review, through an application to a sheriff (s.60(7)). No CPO can remain in force beyond the eighth working day after implementation (ss.60(6) and 65(2)). Usually a children's hearing will be arranged for that day. At that hearing, if it is believed that the child should remain in a place of safety, the hearing may grant a warrant authorising this (ss.66(1) and 69(7)). At a later hearing, what should happen to the child in the longer term will be considered. Children's hearings are discussed in Ch.7.

Emergency protection where a CPO is not available

It is possible, particularly in rural areas, that no sheriff is on hand to consider an application for a CPO. For this reason, two short-term measures provide for emergency protection of children. First, a justice of the peace may consider an application for a CPO where it is not practicable for the application to be made to a sheriff (s.61(1)–(4)). A CPO granted by a justice of the peace has much the same effect as a CPO granted by a sheriff. Secondly, a police officer may, without authorisation from a sheriff, take a child to a place of safety where the officer has reasonable cause to believe that the conditions for making a CPO are satisfied, that it is not practicable to make an application to a sheriff, and that it is necessary in order to protect a child from significant harm (s.61(5)). In each case, a child may not be kept at a place of safety for longer than 24 hours and it is envisaged that a CPO will be applied for, if necessary, within that time.

Permanence order

Permanence orders are a creation of the Adoption and Children (Scotland) Act 2007. Previously, there were two mechanisms designed to facilitate planning a permanent future ("permanency planning") for a child who could not live with his or her parents. The first, the parental responsibilities order (PRO), enabled the local authority to apply to a court to have parental responsibilities and parental rights removed from a child's parents and vested in itself. The second, the "freeing procedure", freed the child for adoption into a new family, often in the face of opposition from at least one of the child's parents. Both orders had been found, for different reasons, to be inadequate in meeting the needs of the children they were designed to serve.

Thus, the Adoption Policy Review Group (see Ch.4) recommended the abolition of PROs and the freeing procedure and the creation of a new order, the permanence order (PO). The PO is designed to deal with permanency planning for a range of children – in particular, some who will be adopted and some who will not – so the component parts of a permanence order will vary. They are as follows:

- *The mandatory provision*

Every PO will vest the right to regulate the child's residence and the responsibility to provide guidance to the child in the local authority (s.81).

- *Ancillary provisions*

A PO may do a wide range of other things, including, vesting any of the remaining parental responsibilities and parental rights in the local authority or another person; extinguishing the parental responsibilities or parental rights of a parent or guardian; specifying the arrangements for contact between the child and any other person; and determining any question which has arisen in respect of parental responsibilities, parental rights or "any other aspect of the welfare of the child" (s.82).

- *A condition granting authority for the child to be adopted*

A PO may grant authority for the child to be adopted (s.83).

Only a local authority may apply to a court for a permanence order (s.80 (1)). Where the local authority is seeking a permanence order containing only the mandatory and ancillary provisions (i.e. not authority for the child to be adopted), parents, guardians and others are entitled to notice of the making of the application and other relevant information (s.104(2)–(5)). Thereafter, they merely have the right to "make representations" in respect of the application (s.86(1)). Where the child's father has never had parental responsibilities or parental rights – and "if he can be found" – he must be notified only of the fact of the application and date and place of the hearing (s.104(2)(b)). It is only where the permanence order will include authority for adoption of the child that either parental consent must be forthcoming or it must be dispensed with by the court on one of the limited grounds that justify dispensing with consent to adoption (s.83(1)(c)). However, the consent of a child aged twelve or over is required before any permanence order, whether there is provision for adoption or not, may be made and there is no scope for a court to dispense with the consent of such a child, save in the exceptional case of a child who is incapable of consenting (s.84(1) and (2)).

Before making a permanence order, the sheriff must be satisfied either that there is no person who has the right to determine the child's residence or that the child living with that person is or would be "seriously detrimental to child's welfare" (s.84(5)(c)). Thereafter, consideration of granting a permanence order is subject to the fundamental principles of child law: the paramountcy of the child's welfare, the child's right to participate and presumed non-intervention (s.84(3)–(5)).

Liability for errors
To what extent will a local authority and others, like health care professionals, be liable in damages for errors, whether the error results in a failure to act timeously and appropriately or in over-zealous intervention? At one time, the local authority was largely protected against claims for breach of statutory duty or negligence (*X v Bedfordshire County Council* (1995); *M v Newham London Borough Council* (1995)). The European Court of Human Rights stepped in to limit this privileged position (*Z v United Kingdom* (2002); *TP and KM v United Kingdom* (2002); *E v United* Kingdom (2003)). However, litigants continue to face obstacles in securing damages. For wrongly-accused parents, there is the problem that the House of Lords has been reluctant to view them as being owed a duty of care by local authorities and health care professionals acting in good faith (*JD v East Berkshire Community Health, MAK v Dewsbury Healthcare NHS Trust and RK v Oldham NHS Trust* (2005)). For adults who were abused as children, their difficulty may be that they delay too long in raising the action and find it time barred (*Bowden v Poor Sisters of Nazareth; Whitton v Poor Sisters of Nazareth* (2008)).

OTHER MECHANISM DESIGNED TO PROTECT CHILDREN (AND OTHERS)

The criminal law
Children receive much the same general protection as is afforded to everyone by the criminal law. Thus, killing a child will be murder or culpable homicide. Striking a child will normally constitute assault. However – and only in the context of a child-victim – Scots law countenances "justifiable assault" (Criminal Justice (Scotland) Act 2003 ss.51–53). This invidious concept permits a parent (and a limited range of others) charged with assaulting his or her own child to advance a defence that the action was "physical punishment carried out in the exercise of a parental right" and was justifiable. An assault will never be justifiable if it involved a blow to the head, shaking or the use of an implement (s.51(3)). In other cases, in addressing whether it was justifiable, the court is directed to consider the nature of what was done; the reason for it and the

circumstances in which it took place; its duration and frequency; the physical or mental effect on the child; the child's age; and the child's personal characteristics including, but not limited to, the child's sex and state of health (s.51(1)). In addition, it may consider other relevant factors (s.51(2)).

Statute intervened long ago to create specific offences that may only be committed in respect of child-victims. Thus, anyone who neglects or ill-treats a child under the age of 16 in his or her care commits an offence (Children and Young Persons (Scotland) Act 1937 s.12). There are a host of sexual offences that may only be committed in respect of children in particular age groups (Criminal Law (Consolidation) Act 1995).

Protecting children from sexual exploitation has resulted in a number of legislative initiatives, albeit not all of the initiatives are designed to protect only children. Certain sex offenders are required to register with the police upon their release from prison and to update their contact information for a specific period of time or for the remainder of their life, depending on their sentence (Sexual Offences Act 2003 ss.80 *et seq*). As yet in the UK, there is no blanket notification to the public of such an offender's presence in the area, but the police may notify specific persons, like a potential employer, in certain circumstances (*M v Chief Constable, Strathclyde Police* (2003)). In addition, a "qualifying offender" may be subject to a sexual offences prevention order (SOPO), requiring him or her to desist from certain conduct, like contacting a victim or living in a household with a person under the age of 16 (Sexual Offences Act 2003 s.105; Protection of Children and Prevention of Sexual Offences (Scotland) Act 2005 s.17(4)). Breach of a SOPO is an offence it itself. The 2005 Act s.1, created a new offence of meeting (or attempting to meet) a child with the intention of engaging in unlawful sexual activity, designed to combat the "grooming" of potential victims, particularly via the Internet. Section 2 of the 2005 Act enables a chief constable to apply for a risk of sexual harm order (RSHO) where an individual has engaged in specified acts on at least two occasions and the order is necessary "for the purpose of protecting children generally or any child from harm" (whether physical or psychological) from the perpetrator. Criminal conduct is not an essential precondition for a RSHO to be granted, but breach of the order is again an offence.

Persons disqualified or barred from working with children (and other vulnerable people)

Fears about the safety of children are not confined to sex offenders and, where a person has endangered a child in the past, there is a question mark over his or her suitability to have charge of children in the future. The Protection of Children (Scotland) Act 2003 was passed to provide for a centralised system of recording information about individuals disqualified from working with children and a prohibition on their seeking work with children once disqualified. When the Protection of Vulnerable Groups (Scotland) Act 2007 comes into force, the original system will be replaced by a much broader scheme. It will result in the creation of a "Children's List" and an "Adults' List" (persons barred from working with children or vulnerable adults respectively), the vetting of everyone who seeks to work with children (defined as a person under the age of 18) or other vulnerable people, the barring of listed persons from relevant "regulated work" and the sharing of information between agencies.

Further reading:
E.E. Sutherland, *Child and Family Law*, 2nd edn (W. Green, 2008), Ch.9; *Getting It Right for Every Child* (GIRFEC) website at: *http://www.scotland.gov.uk/Topics/People/Young-People/childrensservices/girfec* [accessed June 25, 2008].

7. THE CHILDREN'S HEARINGS SYSTEM

The children's hearings system has now been operating in Scotland for just under 40 years. Resulting from the recommendations of the *Report of the Committee on Children and Young Persons* (1964) (known as "the Kilbrandon Report"), it is founded on three principles:
- that children who "were wronged" could be accommodated in the same system as "children who did wrong";
- that both groups of children should receive intervention in their lives, where appropriate, on the basis of "treatment";
- that while courts may be the appropriate forum in which to determine disputed facts, the decision on what to do for the child thereafter could be dealt with more effectively by panels of lay persons.

While aspects of the hearings system have been criticised, re-examined and reformed, this remains the philosophy today. The Children (Scotland) Act 1995 now governs the way the system operates and references in this chapter are to that Act unless otherwise stated. The system underwent its most recent major review as part of *Getting It Right for Every Child* (see Ch.6) and proposals for reform were advanced in the Draft Children's Services (Scotland) Bill (2005). As with the rest of that Bill, the current Scottish government is reassessing it and will make fresh reform proposals in due course.

Management and organisation
While overall responsibility for the children's hearings system lies with the Scottish Ministers (s.42), it is organised through the Scottish Children's Reporter Administration (SCRA) and Children's Panel Advisory

Committees (CPACs). SCRA appoints and manages the deployment of individual reporters throughout Scotland. While the 1995 Act talks in terms of the responsibilities of the Principal Reporter, the chief executive of SCRA, the work is carried out on a day-to-day basis by individual reporters across Scotland. CPACs, appointed by each local authority, advise on the appointment of the panel members, the lay people who make decisions in individual cases. It can be anticipated that SCRA, the CPACs and other parts of the hearings infrastructure will soon be brought together under one administrative umbrella.

How a child comes into the system

Reporters are central to the operation of the system, since it is their function to receive information about children who may be in need of compulsory measures of supervision, to investigate the case, to decide whether a hearing should be convened and, if so, to arrange a hearing (s.53). Information comes from a variety of sources, with most referrals coming from the police and the local authority. However, anyone may refer a case to the reporter. In addition, the courts have specific powers to do so (s.54).

Having received a report, it is the duty of the reporter to investigate the case and he or she will call upon other agencies, like the local authority, to provide additional information. In order to justify a hearing, the reporter must be satisfied of two things:
- that there is a *prima facie* case establishing one of the grounds of referral (discussed below), and
- that compulsory measures of supervision may be necessary (s.56).

The grounds of referral

Section 52(2) of the 1995 Act uses the term "conditions" when indicating the grounds on which a child can be referred to a children's hearing apart from direct references from a court. However, they are universally known as the "grounds of referral". They are that:

(a) the child is beyond the control of any relevant person.

(b) the child is falling into bad associations or is exposed to moral danger.
This ground may be satisfied by the child's own conduct, like "hanging out with a bad crowd", or by conditions in the home, like the presence of drug addicts.

(c) the child is likely due to a lack of parental care (i) to suffer unnecessarily; or (ii) to be impaired seriously in his or her health or development.
While the term "parental care" is used, the reference is to a lack of care by anyone responsible for the child, whether a parent or not. It is not necessary that the lack of care should be motivated by malice or indifference. For example, where a mother erroneously, but sincerely, believed her son to be

autistic and insisted on him attending a special school the ground was held to be satisfied (*R v Grant* (2000)).

(d) the child is a child in respect of whom any offence mentioned in Schedule 1 to the Criminal Procedure (Scotland) Act 1995 has been committed.

Broadly, the specified offences are sexual offences, offences involving neglect of the child (exposing the child to various hazards) and offences relating to female genital mutilation.

(e) the child is, or is likely to become, a member of the same household as a child in respect of whom any of the offences referred to in paragraph (d) above has been committed.

This simply refers back to the ground above and enables all the children in a family to be considered where one child has been a victim of a specified offence.

(f) the child is, or is likely to become, a member of the same household as a person who has committed any of the offences referred to in paragraph (d) above.

Again, this refers back to the specified offences and is designed to protect all children who might become part of the same household as the perpetrator of such an offence.

(g) the child is, or is likely to become, a member of the same household as a person in respect of whom an offence under ss.1–3 of the Criminal Law (Consolidation) (Scotland) Act 1995 (incest and intercourse with a child by a step-parent or a person in a position of trust) has been committed by a person in that household.

Again, this ground seeks to protect children who might become part of the same household as a particular type of victim who lives with an offender, in this case, a person convicted of incest or intercourse in breach of trust.

(h) the child has failed to attend school regularly without reasonable excuse.

Truancy is a ground of referral, whether it is a matter of the child's choice or because a parent failed to send the child to school or make other appropriate arrangements.

(i) the child has committed an offence.

Since Scots law sets the age of criminal responsibility at eight, only a child of this age or older can satisfy this ground (Criminal Procedure (Scotland) Act 1995 s.41). Since 2005, rather than convene a hearing, the reporter now has the option of referring a suitable offender to the Restorative Justice Service (see below). In addition, pilot projects have been established in a number of areas to try out "fast track" hearings for persistent offenders.

*(j) the child has misused alcohol or any drug, whether or not a
controlled drug within the meaning of the Misuse of Drugs Act 1971.*
It should be noted that it is the *misuse*, rather than the *use*, of alcohol or
drugs that is relevant here.

*(k) the child has misused a volatile substance by deliberately inhaling its
vapour, other than for medicinal purposes.*
This ground was introduced in 1983 to deal with the problem of "glue
sniffing" and other misuse of volatile substances.

*(l) the child is being provided with accommodation by a local authority
under section 25 ... and ... his or her behaviour is such that special
measures are necessary for his or her adequate supervision in his or her
interest or the interest of others.*
Where a local authority is looking after a child, it may be that the child's
behaviour is such that the local authority believes additional measures,
including the use of secure accommodation, may be necessary in order to
protect the child from his or her own actions or to protect others from the
child's conduct. This ground enables such additional measures to be
considered and, if necessary, authorised.

*(m) a requirement is made of the Principal Reporter under section 11(1)
of the Antisocial Behaviour etc (Scotland) Act 2004 (power of the sheriff
to require the Principal Reporter to refer the case to a children's
hearing) in respect of the child's case and the child is not subject to a
supervision requirement*
This ground was added by the Antisocial Behaviour etc (Scotland) Act
2004, the statute that extended the application of anti-social behaviour
orders (ASBOs) to young people in the 12–15 age group. Where so directed
by a sheriff, the reporter has no discretion over arranging a hearing. To
date, ASBOs have been little used in respect of young people under 16 in
Scotland.

Arranging a hearing
Where the reporter is satisfied that there is a *prima facie* case establishing
one or more of the grounds of referral and that compulsory measures of
supervision may be necessary (i.e. that other arrangements will not be
sufficient), he or she will arrange a hearing. The three panel members who
will constitute the particular hearing will be notified of the time, date and
place of the hearing and will be provided with copies of the relevant
background documents. "Relevant persons" (see Ch.6) receive similar
notification and, as a result of reforms introduced in response to criticism
from the European Court of Human Rights (*McMichael v United Kingdom*
(1995)), now also receive copies of the relevant documents (s.45(8) and
(9)). The child is entitled to receive notification in writing of the time, date
and place of the hearing and of his or her right and obligation to attend
(s.45(1)). As a result of a human rights challenge, this time before a
domestic court (*S v Miller* (2001)), a child of 12 or over now normally

receives the relevant documents as well, although there is scope for withholding documents from a child in certain circumstances including the likely distress to the child of discovering previously-unknown information. A child under 12 will not receive a full set of documents unless a request for them is made by the child or his or her representative. Prior to the hearing, the reporter may arrange a business meeting with three panel members to discuss procedural and other administrative matters (s.64).

The hearing—those who may be present and their functions

The conduct of the hearing is a matter for the chairperson of each hearing and he or she is directed to permit attendance only by persons whose presence is necessary for the proper consideration of the case and to take all reasonable steps to keep the number of persons present to a minimum (s.43). However, certain persons have a right to attend the particular hearing, others have a right to attend hearings generally, and yet others may attend with the permission of the chairperson.

The child and the relevant persons (often the child's parents) are entitled, and usually obliged, to attend the hearing (s.45). A genetic father, who is not also a relevant person, has a right (but no obligation) to attend, provided that he is living with the child's mother. Obviously, the three panel members selected to serve on a particular hearing will be present, as will the reporter, since he or she is obliged to make a record of the proceedings. Any safeguarder appointed by the hearing will usually be present. A safeguarder is an independent person appointed by the children's hearing or a sheriff to protect and promote the child's interests (s.41). Given the local authority's duty to provide a social background report and to implement decisions of the hearing (s.71), a social worker is usually present and is likely to participate in discussions.

The child and each relevant person may be accompanied by a person to assist them at the hearing. In the past, the absence of legal aid to pay for representation at hearings meant that lawyers rarely appeared. Again, as a result of the human rights challenge raised in *S v Miller* (2001), a representative may be appointed to the child where his or her liberty is at stake. Legal aid is now more widely available to pay for representation (subject to eligibility) of relevant persons at hearings.

The right of journalists to be present at a hearing is subject to the hearing's power to exclude them (s.43(3) and (4)) and extensive restrictions on reporting anything that would identify any child involved in the case (s.44(1)). Members of the Council on Tribunals, or its Scottish Committee, have the right to attend a hearing, subject to the hearing's power to exclude them (s.43(3) and (4)). A host of other persons may be permitted to attend a hearing at the chairman's discretion. The child's school teacher, for example, may have a valuable contribution to make and may be permitted to be present.

The hearing—explaining the grounds of referral

The first thing the chairperson of the hearing must do, after introducing those present and explaining the purpose of the hearing, is to explain the grounds of referral to the child and the relevant persons. Since it is only where the child and the relevant persons accept the grounds of referral that the hearing can proceed, this is of immense importance (s.64(1)). The child and the relevant persons must then be asked if they accept the grounds of referral and, depending on their responses, various things can happen.

If the child does not understand the grounds of referral, the hearing can either discharge the referral or direct the reporter to apply to the sheriff for a finding as to whether any of the grounds of referral is established (s.65(9)). The decision is determined by the welfare principle (s.16). Once discharged, no further action can be taken in relation to that ground of referral. Where the child or any of the relevant persons do not accept the grounds of referral, the hearing can, again, either discharge the referral or direct the reporter to apply to the sheriff for a finding as to whether any of the grounds of referral is established (s.65(7)(a)). Where the child or the relevant persons accept only part of the grounds of referral, the hearing can proceed in respect of those grounds (s.65(6)), or it can discharge the referral, or direct the reporter to apply to the sheriff for a finding as to whether any of the grounds of referral is established (s.65(7)(b)). Where the child and the relevant persons accept the grounds of referral as stated, the hearing proceeds to the next stage (s.65(5)). Throughout the proceedings of a children's hearing, the panel members must bear in mind that it may be necessary to appoint a safeguarder and, if so, to make such an appointment (s.41).

Application to the sheriff
Where grounds of referral are not understood by the child or not accepted by the child or any of the relevant persons, the hearing may direct the reporter to apply to the sheriff for a finding as to whether any of the grounds of referral is established. Where the reporter has lodged an application, it must be heard by the sheriff within 28 days (s.68(2)). Proof is on the balance of probabilities, except where it is alleged that the child has committed an offence, in which case proof beyond reasonable doubt is required (s.68(3)). The child is entitled and is usually obliged to attend the proof (s.68(4) and (5)). Relevant persons also have a right to attend and the child and the relevant persons may be represented, with legal aid being available to fund representation (s.68(4)). In addition, the sheriff must consider whether it is necessary to appoint a safeguarder for the child (s.41).

Where the sheriff finds that none of the grounds of referral has been established, he or she must dismiss the application and discharge the referral (s.8(9)). Where the sheriff finds any of the grounds of referral to have been established, he or she will remit the case back to the reporter to arrange for a hearing to determine the case (s.68(10)(a)).

The hearing—consideration of the case
Where the grounds of referral are accepted by the child and the relevant persons or are established before the sheriff, the hearing moves on to consider the case. In the case of accepted grounds, the whole process will often be continuous. The hearing considers not only the grounds of referral

but also any available reports, including social background reports, and other relevant information (s.69(1)). It is of the essence of the hearings system that everyone involved should have the opportunity to participate freely in seeking a positive way forward for the child and the hearing is directed to discuss the case with the child, the relevant persons, any representative and any safeguarder.

Exclusion of a relevant person
The 1995 Act introduced the possibility of temporarily excluding a relevant person (s.46), acknowledging that a child's right to participate in his or her own hearing might be inhibited by the presence of a particular adult. Exclusion is permitted in two situations: either it must be necessary in order to obtain the child's views; or the person's presence must be causing, or be likely to cause, significant distress to the child. A relevant person's representative may also be excluded from the hearing. Once the excluded person returns to the hearing, the chairperson is obliged to explain to him or her the substance of what has taken place during the period of exclusion.

The hearing's decision
Having considered the case fully, the hearing will then decide on the appropriate disposal of the case. The disposal must be made in the light of the welfare principle and the following options are open to the hearing:

- *Continue the case*
The hearing may be continued to a later date, where, for example, the hearing members require further information (s.69(2)).

- *Discharge the referral*
Unless the hearing is satisfied that the child is in need of compulsory measures of supervision, it must discharge the referral and all orders, requirements and warrants issued in connection with the ground of referral so discharged cease to have effect (s.69(1)(b), (12) and (13)).

- *Refer the case to the Restorative Justice Service (RJS)*
The RJS was established in 2005 and offers the young person the opportunity to confront, and seek to make amends for, his or her offending behaviour. As we have seen, the reporter may divert the case of an offender to the RJS and the hearing itself may also do so. In either case, there is a rigorous procedure for assessing the "suitability" of the young person and both the young person and the victim must agree to participate in a restorative justice programme.

- *Make a supervision requirement*
Where the hearing is satisfied that the child is in need of compulsory measures of supervision, it will make a supervision requirement (s.69(1)(c)). The nature of the supervision requirement is governed by the welfare principle (s.16(1)). The child may be required to live at a specified place (s.70(3)(a)). While a hearing may decide that a child should live with

his or her parents, the power to require a child to live at a specified place is very wide-ranging indeed, and may mean that the child goes to live with other relatives, foster carers or in a residential establishment. The decision of a hearing supersedes any court order governing the child's residence (*Aitken v Aitken* (1978)). The hearing has the power to impose any other condition that is consistent with the general principles of Part II of the 1995 Act (s.70(3)(a)). Any condition must be stated in unambiguous language along with the reasons for its imposition. Punishment forms no part of the hearings system and conditions must be aimed at meeting the child's welfare needs.

While not limiting the range of conditions a hearing may make, the Act mentions two possible conditions. The first requires the child to submit to any medical examination or treatment (s.70(5)(a)). However, the hearing has no power to impose a condition which would limit the child's general right to consent to or refuse such treatment where the child is of sufficient maturity to understand what it involves (s.90). The second condition mentioned allows the hearing to regulate the child's contact with any specified person or class of persons (s.70(5)(b)). The hearing may also require that the place where the child is to live should not be disclosed to a specified person or class of persons (s.70(6)) or require that the supervision requirement shall be reviewed at a particular time (s.70(7)).

- *Impose a movement restriction condition*

This option was added by the Antisocial Behaviour etc (Scotland) Act 2004 (adding s.70 (9A)(b) to the 1995 Act) and it is anticipated that it will be used most often to subject the young person to what is, effectively, a curfew, by requiring him or her to stay at a specified place during certain hours (e.g. at home between 6pm and 6am). However, it could be used to require the young person to stay *away* from a specified place. In addition to movement restriction, the young person may be required "to comply with such arrangements for monitoring compliance with the restrictions" as are specified (s.70(11)) and this could include electronic monitoring ("tagging").

Implementing the hearing's decision

A local authority has a statutory duty to give effect to a supervision requirement imposed by a children's hearing (s.71). There have been problems in the past when local authorities sometimes failed to do so, often because of a lack of resources. As a result, the 1995 Act was amended and now provides a procedure whereby the reporter, having given notice to the local authority, may apply to the sheriff for an enforcement order, directing the local authority to perform its statutory duty (ss.70(7A)–(7E) and 71A). In addition (and without any special procedure), where any hearing concludes that a local authority is failing in its obligation to provide education to a child excluded from school, it may require the reporter to refer the matter to the Scottish Ministers (s.75B).

Appeals

Appeals from the decision of a children's hearing are infrequent. However, the child and any relevant person has standing to appeal, whether or not the person actually attended the hearing (s.51(1)), as does the child's safeguarder. Legal aid is available to fund representation for an appeal. The reporter may not appeal against the decision of a hearing. The appeal must be lodged within three weeks, beginning with the date of the hearing's decision (s.51(1)) and the date assigned for hearing the appeal must be no more than 28 days after the appeal was lodged.

At the outset, and throughout the appeal, the sheriff must consider whether it is necessary to appoint a safeguarder (s.41). The sheriff is directed to allow the appeal if he or she is satisfied that the hearing's decision is "not justified in all the circumstances of the case" (s.51(5)). Since all the circumstances of the case are relevant, the sheriff is entitled to consider changes in circumstances that have occurred since the hearing. In considering the appeal, the sheriff may hear evidence from the parties or their representatives. In addition, he or she may examine the reporter and the compilers of any reports, and call for any further reports that may be of assistance (s.51(3)).

Having heard all the evidence, the sheriff will allow or dismiss the appeal. If the appeal is dismissed, the sheriff must confirm the decision of the hearing (s.51(4)). If the sheriff allows the appeal, he or she may remit the case back to the hearing, with reasons for allowing the appeal, so that the hearing can reconsider the case (s.51(5)(c)(i)); or discharge the child from any further hearing in relation to the grounds of referral (s.51(5)(c)(ii)); or substitute any disposal that the children's hearing could have made without any need to refer the case back to a hearing (s.51(5)(c)(iii)).

Further appeal lies by way of stated case from the sheriff direct to the Court of Session or to the sheriff principal (and, with leave from the sheriff principal, to the Court of Session), on a point of law or in respect of any irregularity in the conduct of the case (s.51(11)). Such appeals are open to the child, any relevant person, the safeguarder, and the reporter on behalf of the children's hearing (s.51(12)) and the application to state a case for the purpose of the appeal must be made within 28 days of the decision being made (s.51(13)). There is no appeal to the House of Lords (s.51(11)(b)).

Review of established grounds of referral—new evidence

Very occasionally, new evidence may emerge which casts doubt on grounds of referral which have been established. As a result of what came to be known as the *"Ayrshire Case"* (*L, Petitioners (No.1)* and *(No.2)* (1993)), the 1995 Act introduced a provision for dealing with new evidence relating to the grounds of referral which is available in the following, very limited, circumstances:

- Challenging established grounds of referral is available only to the child and the relevant persons (s.85(4));
- The grounds under challenge must have been established before the sheriff (s.85(2));

- The applicant must claim (i) to have evidence that was not considered by the sheriff in the original application and which might have materially affected that application; (ii) that this evidence is likely to be credible and reliable and would have been admissible in respect of the original application; and (iii) that there is a reasonable explanation of the failure to lead the evidence during the original application (s.85(3)).

If the sheriff is not satisfied that the claims made are established, he or she must dismiss the application and the hearing's disposal stands (s.85(5)). Where the sheriff is satisfied that the claims made in the application for review are established, there are two possibilities. Either, the challenge is such that all of the grounds of referral are struck down by it, or, while some of the grounds are no longer established, others remain valid. Where any ground of referral remains established, the sheriff may remit the case to the reporter to arrange a hearing and, pending the hearing, may order that the child be kept in a place of safety (s.85(6)(b)). Where none of the original grounds remains established there is no longer any valid reason for a supervision requirement unless new grounds are established (s.85(7)(b)). However, the Act acknowledges that it might be precipitate simply to return the child to the family without any arrangements for transition. Thus, while the sheriff may terminate the supervision requirement immediately, he or she may also postpone such termination (s.85(7)(a)).

Review of the supervision requirement
Unless a supervision requirement is reviewed within one year of its being made, it ceases to have effect (s.73(2)). Where a child is subject to a supervision requirement, the local authority must refer a case to the reporter for review where it is satisfied, either, that the requirement ought to cease to have effect or be varied or that a condition contained in the requirement is not being complied with; or the best interests of the child would be served by their applying for a permanence order (or variation, amendment or revocation thereof) or placing the child for adoption (s.73(4)). The child or any relevant person may apply for review of a supervision requirement at any time three months after, either, the date when the requirement was made or the date of the most recent continuation or review of a requirement (s.73(6)).

A hearing to review a supervision requirement operates much like the original hearing and can continue the review hearing to allow for further investigation, terminate the supervision requirement, vary the requirement, insert in the requirement any other requirement it could have made, or continue the requirement (s.73(9)).

Further reading:
E.E. Sutherland, *Child and Family Law*, 2nd edn (W. Green, 2008), Ch.10; K. McK. Norrie, *Children's Hearings in Scotland,* 2nd edn (W. Green, 2005).

8. GETTING INTO INTIMATE ADULT RELATIONSHIPS

Adults live in many different kinds of intimate relationships. For different-sex couples the main options are marriage or non-marital cohabitation, with just under 30,000 couples getting married in Scotland each year. For same-sex couples the options are civil partnership or simple cohabitation, with over 1,000 couples registering civil partnerships in 2006, the first full year after registration became possible. The legal system lays down clear rules for entry into marriage and civil partnership. Cohabitation outwith one of these relationships has increased in popularity, with cohabiting couples being more open about the nature of their relationship than they were in the past.

COHABITATION

While most spouses and civil partners cohabit, "cohabitation proper" is the state in which a couple live together quite openly, without any pretence that they are, in fact, spouses or civil partners. One difficulty the legal system has with cohabitation is how to define it. How long do the parties have to live together before they are regarded as cohabiting? What should be their level of commitment? Does it matter whether they are raising children together? As we will see in Ch.9, where the law does recognise cohabitation for a particular purpose, like presumed co-ownership of household goods, it couches its definition in terms of a marriage-like or a civil partnership-like relationship. A second problem arises over the reasons that people cohabit. Given that some couples cohabit as an express rejection of a more formal relationship, should their choice be respected by allowing them to avoid the consequences of marriage or civil partnership? Is that fair to couples who have lived together for a long time and, perhaps, had children? There is little legal regulation of who may cohabit, apart from the general provisions of the criminal law on the age of consent to sexual activity and incest. There are no formalities to be observed for a couple to cohabit.

IRREGULAR MARRIAGE

The expression "common law marriage" is used, somewhat loosely and erroneously, in lay circles and the media to denote a cohabitation relationship. Until it was prospectively and substantially abolished by the Family Law (Scotland) Act 2006 s.3(1), Scots law recognised one form of irregular marriage—marriage by cohabitation with habit and repute. At common law, such a marriage required all of the following conditions to be satisfied:

- The couple must have lived together as husband and wife, rather than as lovers, employer and housekeeper, or what the older cases describe as "man and mistress".
- The cohabitation must have been in Scotland.
- The cohabitation must have been for a sufficiently long time. It was emphasised consistently that there was no hard and fast rule on duration and that it was the quality of the cohabitation and repute that mattered. While lengthy periods of cohabitation were often involved, some cases accepted periods of cohabitation of less than a year as being sufficient (*Shaw v Henderson* (1982) (11 months); *Mullen v Mullen* (1991) (six months)).
- The parties must have been reputed to be husband and wife and "although repute need not be universal it must be general, substantially unvarying and consistent and not divided" (*Low v Gorman* (1970), p.359).
- The parties must have had capacity to marry. If there was an impediment, like a pre-existing marriage, at the beginning of the cohabitation, that was later removed by divorce, the clock could only begin to run from the date of the divorce (*Shaw v Henderson* (1982)).

Where such a marriage was claimed to exist, it was usual to seek a declarator of marriage in the Court of Session and sometimes this was sought after the death of one of the parties to enable the survivor to claim succession rights. Once recognised, such a marriage had all the effects of a regular marriage. The concept was criticised for rewarding deceptions and creating uncertainty and the Scottish Law Commission recommended its prospective abolition (Report on Family Law (1992) Rec.42). In addition, the modern tendency to be open about the fact that the couple were simply cohabiting limited the scope for its application (*S v S* (2006)).

Two caveats to the statutory abolition of the concept should be noted. First, abolition was of prospective effect only, so the issue of such marriages will arise for many years to come. For a marriage by cohabitation by habit and repute to be protected against the concept's prospective abolition, "the cohabitation with habit and repute" must have

- ended before s.3(1) came into force (4 May 2006),
- begun before, but ended after, s.3(1) came into force, or
- begun before s.3(1) came into force and continue thereafter (2006 Act s.3(2)).

Secondly, the concept lingers on as a cure for defective foreign marriages where one of the parties has died, provided that the following conditions are satisfied:

- one of the parties has died domiciled in Scotland, and
- the surviving partner is domiciled in Scotland, and
- the parties "purported to enter a marriage" outwith the United Kingdom before the cohabitation with habit and repute began (2006 Act s.3(3) and (4)).

ENGAGEMENT TO MARRY

Actions for breach of promise of marriage were abolished in 1984 (Law Reform (Husband and Wife) (Scotland) Act 1984 s.1(1)). However, where property was transferred by one party to the other in contemplation of marriage, such property can be recovered if the marriage does not take place (*Shilliday v Smith* (1998)). Engagement rings have presented a particular problem where the marriage has not gone ahead. In one case, the court regarded the ring as an unconditional gift, and the woman was allowed to keep it (*Gold v Hume* (1950)) while, in another case, it was treated as a conditional gift, and the man who had given it was entitled to get it back (*Savage v McAllister* (1952)).

REGULAR MARRIAGE—RESTRICTIONS

Since the legal system has always treated marriage as being important, there is extensive regulation of who may marry. Some restrictions can be seen as protecting the individuals involved. Thus, a marriage may be void where one of the parties was coerced into entering it. Other restrictions, like the prohibition on marriage between people who are closely related, express a more general, societal, interest in marriage. The main statute governing marriage is the Marriage (Scotland) Act 1977 and references below are to that Act unless otherwise stated.

Age

The 1977 Act takes a two-pronged approach to the issue of age. First, it provides that no person domiciled in Scotland may marry before reaching the age of 16, regardless of where the marriage takes place (1977 Act s.1(1)). Domicile is the link between an individual and a legal system and where a domiciled Scot goes through a ceremony of marriage abroad before his or her sixteenth birthday, the marriage will not be recognised here, regardless of what the law of the other country might permit. Secondly, the 1977 Act provides that a marriage solemnised in Scotland, where either of the parties is under 16, shall be void (1977 Act s.1(2)). Once a person reaches the age of 16, he or she has the capacity to marry and parental consent (or opposition) is irrelevant.

Male and female

For a valid marriage, the parties must be respectively male and female, with civil partnership being the compromise solution reached at present for same-sex couples. A purported marriage between parties of the same sex will be void (1977 Act s.5(4)(e)). Unlike the position in the past (*X, Petitioner* (1957); *Corbett v Corbett* (1971)), Scots law now provides a procedure for a person to be recognised as being of the gender other than that appearing on his or her original birth certificate provided that certain conditions are satisfied and, once a full gender recognition certificate is issued, a person may marry in his or her acquired gender (Gender Recognition Act 2004). Where gender recognition is sought by a married person, the procedure cannot be completed until he or she divorces (Gender Recognition Act 2004 s.4; Divorce (Scotland) Act 1976 s.1(1)(b)). There is an expedited procedure enabling former spouses to register a civil partnership if the parties so wish (Civil Partnership Act 2004 s.96), something the European Court has found to be a satisfactory solution to the parties' art.12 rights under the European Convention on Human Rights (*R and F v United Kingdom* (2006)). Where same-sex partners marry abroad the marriage will not be recognised as such in the United Kingdom (*Wilkinson v Kitzinger* (2006)), but it may be recognised as a "specified relationship" and accorded the same status as a civil partnership (Civil Partnership Act 2004 Sch.20).

Prior subsisting marriage or civil partnership
The starting point is that only monogamous marriage is recognised in Scotland: that is, a person may only be married to one spouse at a time. Where one party is already married, any subsequent attempt at marriage is void (1977 Act s.5(4)(b)). Furthermore, anyone who attempts to marry again, in the knowledge that a prior marriage remains valid, commits the offence of bigamy. Where one of the parties to a bigamous marriage was unaware of his or her partner's prior subsisting marriage, the second ceremony creates what is known as a "putative marriage". This is not a marriage in any real sense, but a child born as a result of such a union is deemed in law to be legitimate: something that is of little relevance today since the (purported) abolition of the concept of "illegitimacy" (Family Law (Scotland) Act 2006 s.21). As Scotland became more culturally diverse, the issue of polygamy (usually, a man having more than one wife simultaneously) arose. Initially, Scots law did not recognise polygamous marriages (*Muhammad v Suna* (1956)). Statute intervened long ago to provide recognition of such marriages in certain circumstances (Matrimonial Proceedings (Polygamous Marriages) Act 1972 and the Private International Law (Miscellaneous Provisions) Act 1995 s.7(2)). With the advent of civil partnership, it was necessary to extend the law to provide that being a civil partner precludes entry into a marriage (1977 Act s.5(4)(b)).

Prohibited degrees of relationship
A purported marriage between certain relatives is void. Originally, the prohibitions were derived from the Old Testament (Leviticus, xviii, 6–24) and reinforced by the belief that procreation by close relatives increases the likelihood of genetic defects being passed on to future generations. The modern prohibitions are now contained exclusively in section 2 of, and Schedule 1 to, the 1977 Act, as amended. If a marriage is not within the degrees specified there, it is permitted. Marriage is not allowed between persons who are regarded as being too closely related to each other by reason of a blood relationship (consanguinity), a family relationship through marriage or civil partnership (affinity), or a relationship created by adoption. The prohibitions based on consanguinity reflect the criminal law on incest. Clive gives the following succinct explanation of the detailed prohibitions set out in the Act:

"You cannot marry (a) your parent, grandparent or great grandparent; (b) your child, grandchild or great grandchild; (c) your brother, sister, nephew, niece, uncle or aunt. Relations of the half blood are treated in the same way as relations of the full blood. These are the only blood relations with whom marriage is prohibited. So you can marry your cousin or a remoter relative . . . You cannot marry your former spouse's child or grandchild (or—to put it the other way round—the former spouse of your parent or grandparent), unless: (a) you have both attained the age of 21; and (b) 'the younger party has not at any time before attaining the age of 18 lived in the same household as the other party and been treated by the other party as a child of the family' . . . The above are the only prohibitions based on affinity. It follows that you can marry your former spouse's brother, sister, nephew, niece, uncle, aunt or grandparent . . . You cannot marry your adoptive parent or former adoptive parent, or your adopted child or former adopted child. These are the only prohibitions based on adoption. It follows that you can marry your brother or sister by adoption, provided that no other prohibition applies." (E.M. Clive, *The Law of Husband and Wife in Scotland*, 4th edn (W. Green, 1997), paras 3.006–3.011, footnotes omitted).

It should be noted that the Family Law (Scotland) Act 2006 s.1, removed the restriction on marriage between former parents-in-law and children-in-law.

Consent

Marriage is a consensual relationship: that is, each party must consent freely and with full understanding of what he or she is doing. A substantial body of case law developed under the common law elaborating on what level and form of impaired consent was sufficient to render a marriage void. The Scottish Law Commission recommended clarification of, and amendment to, the then existing law (*Report on Family Law* (1992), Rec.42). The Family Law (Scotland) Act 2006 added s.20A to the 1977 Act to give effect to the recommendations.

A purported marriage will be void where:

- *One party is incapable of understanding the nature of marriage and of consenting to it at the time of the ceremony*

The source of the incapacity is immaterial and may result from a permanent or temporary condition. Mental illness or disability may be sufficient to result in the requisite incapacity. However, in *Long v Long* (1950), a young woman was found to be of limited intelligence but still quite capable of understanding the nature of marriage and of consenting to it. The court made clear that a heavy burden of proof lies on the person seeking to challenge the validity of a marriage. While the effects are temporary, consumption of alcohol or drugs may result in the requisite incapacity.

- *One party gave consent by reason only of duress*

In order to invalidate a marriage, the duress or pressure exerted must have had the effect of making the individual appear to consent when he or she would not have done so but for the influence being exerted. Threats or pressure are not confined to physical harm to the individual "consenting" and can include the threat of imprisonment, social ostracism or harm to another person. There are numerous modern example of the kind of pressure that will suffice here. See, for example, *Mahmood v Mahmood* (1993) (parental threats to disown a wholly-dependent 21 year-old daughter and send her to live in Pakistan, combined with relentless family pressure) and *Sobrah v Khan* (2002) (bride's mother threatened to send her daughter to Pakistan and then commit suicide). Where a forced marriage took place abroad, a Scottish court used the concept of domicile to establish jurisdiction in order to declare the marriage void (*Singh v Singh* (2005)). Mounting evidence that individuals in the UK have been forced into marriage, either here or by being taken abroad for the ceremony, has resulted in legislation being passed for the rest of the country (Forced Marriage (Civil Protection) Act 2007) and the Scottish Government is consulting on the need to legislate for Scotland.

- *One party gave consent by reason only of error*

The statutory amendment puts beyond doubt what was thought to be the case at common law since it is only error as to the nature of the ceremony (for example, believing the ceremony to be one of engagement, rather than marriage) or the identity of the other party (for example, believing oneself to be marrying one identical twin and, in fact, going through the ceremony with the other) that will render a marriage void (1977 Act s.20A(5)). Error as to the other party's qualities or attributed will not have this effect. This is so even where the error results from the other party's fraud. Thus, in *Lang v Lang* (1921), where a woman induced a man to marry her by telling him that he was the father of the child she was expecting, he was unable to reduce the marriage on discovering that she had lied.

Tacit withholding of consent

At common law, where the parties went through what seemed to be a valid ceremony of marriage, but it was established that there was "no true matrimonial consent" on the part of one or both of them, then the marriage was void (*Orlandi v Castelli* (1961), p.120). As a result – and despite considerable judicial disquiet – what were known as "sham marriages" enabled people to use the legal mechanisms to achieve a desired result, like getting round immigration requirements, while avoiding the burdens of marriage later (*Akram v Akram* (1979); *H v H* (2005)). Statute has now amended the law and tacit withholding of consent alone will not render a marriage void (1977 Act s.20A(4)). Registrars are required to report suspected sham marriages to the immigration authorities (Immigration and Asylum Act 1999 s.24).

REGULAR MARRIAGE—FORMALITIES

By laying down formal requirements for marriage, the legal system can, again, be seen as protecting individuals at the same time as expressing a general, societal interest in marriage. So, for example, the requirements relating to celebrants should reduce the risk of "shotgun weddings" and requirements relating to notice and registration enable accurate public records to be kept. Both civil and religious marriage ceremonies are provided for, the 1977 Act expanded the range of religions accommodated and the Marriage (Scotland) Act 2002 amended the 1977 Act to allow a wider range of venues to be used for civil ceremonies. The early formalities are the same for all marriages, with the nature of the marriage only becoming important at the stage of celebration. Advances in technology made possible the submission of documents in electronic form and the Local Electoral Administration and Registration Services (Scotland) Act 2006 amended the 1977 Act to embrace the change.

Notice of intention to marry

Each party intending to marry must submit notice of intention to marry, using a standard form and known as the "marriage notice", to the district registrar in the district where the marriage is to be solemnised (1977 Act s.3(1)). Where the marriage is to take place at sea, in Scottish waters, submission should be to the registrar who will perform the ceremony (civil ceremony) or to any registrar (religious ceremony) (1977 Act s.3(6)(b)). Each marriage notice must be accompanied by:

- the prescribed fee (presently £26);
- a copy of each individual's birth certificate;
- where a person has been a registered civil partner or spouse before, a copy of the decree dissolving the previous relationship or a copy of the previous partner's death certificate (1977 Act s.3(1));
- where a person is not domiciled in the United Kingdom and has not been resident here for at least two years, a "certificate of no known impediment" from the country of his or her domicile, "if practicable"(1977 Act s.3(5)); and
- where the marriage is to be between a step-parent and a step-child, a declaration that the younger person has not lived in household with the elder person prior to reaching the age of 18 and been treated as a child of the family.

If either party is unable to submit any of the required documents, he or she may make a declaration stating that fact and the reasons why it is impracticable for the relevant document to be produced. Where any document submitted to the district registrar is in a language other than English, a certified translation must be submitted along with it (1977 Act s.3(3)). Anyone coming to the UK from a non-European Economic Area country to marry must obtain a "visa for marriage" even if he or she does not intend to remain here after the wedding.

Marriage notice book, the "district list" and the "Scottish list"

On receiving the marriage notice, the district registrar must enter the prescribed particulars in the marriage notice book (1977 Act s.4(1)) and enter the names of the parties and the proposed date of the marriage in the "district list" which is displayed in a conspicuous place at the registration office and remains there until the date for the marriage has passed (1977 Act s.4(2) and (2C)(a)). Any person who claims that he or she might have reason to submit an objection to an intended marriage may inspect the marriage notice book, free of charge, at any time when the registration office is open for public business (1977 Act s.4(3)). The district list is transmitted to the Registrar General for entry in the "Scottish list" of intended marriages, which may be inspected by any person in hard copy or via the Internet (1977 Act s.4(2E)-(2G)).

Objections to a proposed marriage

Prior to a marriage taking place, any person may submit an objection in writing to the district registrar (1977 Act s.5(1)). Minor errors, like the misspelling of a name, can be dealt with by the district registrar with the approval of the Registrar General (1977 Act s.5(2)(a)). Where the objection relates to a more serious matter, like a pre-existing marriage, the district registrar will inform the Registrar General and suspend issuing the marriage schedule, pending consideration of the objection (1977 Act s.5(2)(b)).

The marriage schedule

Once the district registrar has received a marriage notice from each of the parties and is satisfied that no impediment to the marriage exists, or has been so informed by the Registrar General, he or she will complete a marriage schedule (1977 Act s.6(1)). This document serves as the basis for registration of all regular marriages. For a civil marriage, the district registrar simply retains it until the ceremony. In the case of a religious marriage, it is collected by one of the parties (1977 Act s.6(3)) and acts as authority for the celebrant to perform the marriage. Usually, the district registrar may not issue a marriage schedule until 14 days have elapsed since the marriage notices were lodged, although the Registrar General may authorise the district registrar to issue the schedule on an earlier date, if good cause can be shown (1977 Act s.6(4)(a)). In addition, the schedule will not normally be issued more than seven days before the ceremony is due to take place, but, again, the Registrar General may waive this requirement (1977 Act s.6(4)(b)).

Civil marriage

Only district registrars or assistant district registrars appointed by the Registrar General may solemnise a civil marriage (1977 Act ss.8(1)(b) and 17). In the past, the ceremony had to take place at the registration office, with an exception being made where the registrar was satisfied that one of the parties could not attend there due to "serious illness or serious bodily injury" (1977 Act s.18(4)(b)). The Marriage (Scotland) Act 2002 amended the 1977 Act to extend greatly the range of possible wedding venues and marriages may now take place at an "approved location" or in Scottish waters on an "approved vessel" (1977 Act s.18(1)). A procedure is in place for the granting of "period approval" or "temporary approval" of a marriage venue (1977 Act s.18A and the Marriage (Approval of Places) (Scotland) Regulations 2002–2006).

For a valid civil marriage the following persons must be present:

- both parties intending to marry;
- two witnesses "professing to be 16 years of age or over"; and
- the registrar.

The registrar must have the marriage schedule and the prescribed fee (currently £46.50) must have been paid (1977 Act s.19(2)). The registrar explains the nature of the proceedings and impediments to marriage, establishes that the parties know of no such impediment and accept each other as spouses and declares them to be married. After the various declarations have been made, the parties, the witnesses and the celebrant sign the marriage schedule (1977 Act s.19(3)) and the particulars are entered in the register of marriages (1977 Act s.19(4)).

Religious marriage

A religious marriage can be solemnised by a person who is:

- a minister of the Church of Scotland; or
- a minister, clergyman, pastor, priest or other marriage celebrant of a religious body prescribed by regulations made by the Scottish Minister; or
- nominated by some other body as a marriage celebrant and registered as such by the Registrar General under s.9 of the Act; or
- temporarily authorised by the Registrar General under s.12 of the Act (1977 Act s.8(1)(a)).

The ceremony should be performed on the date and at the place specified in the marriage schedule and there is provision for the district registrar to accommodate any change in plans after the schedule has been issued (1977 Act s.6(5)–(7)). Again, the parties intending to marry, two witnesses "professing to be 16 years of age or over", and the celebrant must be present and the celebrant must have been given the marriage schedule (1977 Act s.13(1)). The celebrant must use a form of ceremony recognised by the relevant religious body and must include a declaration by the parties, in the presence of each other and two witnesses, that they accept each other as husband and wife and a declaration by the celebrant, thereafter, that they are husband and wife (1977 Act s.14). Nothing in the ceremony must be inconsistent with these declarations. Immediately after the marriage has been solemnised, the parties, the witnesses and the celebrant sign the marriage schedule (1977 Act s.15(1)). Within three days the parties must deliver the marriage schedule to the registrar or arrange for its delivery (1977 Act s.15(2)) and, on receipt, the registrar will enter the particulars in the register of marriages (1977 Act s.15(3)).

Non-compliance with formalities

The 1977 Act makes clear that failure to comply with certain fundamental requirements, like both parties being at least 16 years old, will render a marriage void. However, non-compliance with the more formal requirements will not invalidate a marriage provided that both parties were present at the ceremony and that the marriage has been registered (1977 Act s.23A). Thus, where these conditions are met, the validity of a marriage cannot be questioned simply because the celebrant was not authorised or one of the witnesses was under age. The lack of a marriage schedule is not a curable defect under s.23A (*Sohrab v Khan* (2002)).

Offences
Section 23A does not affect criminal liability. The 1977 Act provides that various kinds of conduct will constitute offences. These are set out in section 24 and cover such matters as falsification of documents, conducting a marriage ceremony when not authorised to do so and failing to register a marriage.

NON-MARRIAGE AND VOID AND VOIDABLE MARRIAGES
Any of the following will render a marriage void:
- either party being already married or a registered civil partner
- either party being under the age of 16;
- the parties being within the prohibited degrees;
- the parties being of the same sex;
- either party being incapable of understanding the nature of marriage or of consenting thereto; or
- either party purporting to give consent but doing so under duress or error (as defined in the Act).

Strictly speaking, a void marriage is not a marriage at all. However, since there will usually have been a ceremony and registration of the marriage, any person wishing to challenge such a "marriage" should raise an action for declarator of nullity of marriage. Such a declarator may now be sought in either the sheriff court or the Court of Session. Either party may seek declarator, as may anyone with a legitimate interest and such a declarator may be sought after the death of one of the parties (*Scott v Kelly* (1992)). While, as a general rule, a void marriage is treated as not having taken place, there are exceptions. For example, when a court grants decree of declarator of nullity, it has the same powers to make financial provision as it has in granting decree of divorce (Family Law (Scotland) Act 1985, s 17(3)).

In Scotland, the only ground on which a marriage is voidable is that one of the parties was incurably and permanently impotent at the time of the marriage; that is, he or she is unable (whether for physical or psychological reasons) to have full sexual intercourse. Only the parties to a voidable marriage have title to sue and a party may found on his or her own impotency (*F v F* (1945)). The parties themselves may be personally barred from raising the action where, for example, they have adopted a child (*AB v CB* (1961)). A voidable marriage remains valid until declarator of nullity is granted, whereupon the decree has retrospective effect. Again, the court may make financial provision. The Scottish Law Commission recommended that the concept of voidable marriage should be abolished

(Report on Family Law, Recs 49 and 50), but this recommendation was not taken up by the legislature.

REGISTERING A CIVIL PARTNERSHIP

Civil partnerships were created by the Civil Partnership Act 2004 as a marriage-equivalent for same-sex couples and references below are to the 2004 Act. As a result, the requirements in terms of capacity (age, forbidden degrees, single status) and consent (understanding and capacity to consent, no duress or relevant error) mirror those for marriage, allowing for necessary adaptations (e.g. the parties must be of the same sex). Like breach of promise of marriage, breach of promise to register a civil partnership is not actionable (2004 Act s.128). To a large extent, the legal formalities for registering a civil partnership also parallel those for marriage (notice, notice book, publicity, opportunity for objections and civil partnership schedule: 2004 Act ss.88–94). However, such was the controversy, in some quarters, surrounding legal recognition of same-sex relationships that legislators felt the need to sanction some significant – and, arguably, wholly unnecessary – differences:

- A civil partnership may only be created through the civil registration procedure and there is no possibility of a religious ceremony (2004 Act s.85).
- While the provisions on duress and error, in the context of civil partnership, now (broadly) mirror those for marriage (2004 Act s.123, as amended by the Family Law (Scotland) Act 2006), there is no provision in respect of tacit withholding of consent in the civil partnership context.
- There is no equivalent of the certificate of "no known impediment" for civil partnership involving a party from abroad.
- Specific registrars are designated "authorised registrars" for the purpose of registering a civil partnership (2004 Act s.87).
- As for marriage, various venues may be approved for the purpose but, in the case of approval for the registration of a civil partnership, "the place must not be in religious premises" (2004 Act s.93(3))
- The witnesses must "have attained the age of 16" (2004 Act s.85(1)(b)), not simply "profess" that this is the case.
- Since bigamy is a common law offence, the civil partnership equivalent is a statutory creation, it being an offence to register a civil partnership while married or in a civil partnership (2004 Act s.100).
- While a person seeking gender recognition must dissolve his or her civil partnership prior to obtaining a full gender recognition certificate, there is no expedited procedure for such a person to marry his or her former civil partner.
- While a civil partnership may be void for much the same reasons as a marriage may be void (2004 Act ss.86 and 123), there is no provision in the 2004 Act for a voidable Scottish civil partnership, although the concept is relevant to civil partnerships from other jurisdictions (2004 Act s.204).

Further reading:
E. E.Sutherland, *Child and Family Law*, 2nd edn (W. Green, 2008), Chs 11
    and 12;
General Register Office for Scotland website, at: *http://www.gro-
    scotland.gov.uk* [accessed June 25, 2008]

9. THE CONSEQUENCES OF INTIMATE ADULT RELATIONSHIPS

While marriage has fewer legal consequences than it did in the past, a number
of significant effects still attach to it and most of them apply equally to civil
partnership. Simple cohabitation may now have more legal consequences
than it used to, but they remain fewer than for marriage or civil partnership
– a distinction found by the European Court of Human Rights to be
unobjectionable (*Burden v United Kingdom* (2008)). This chapter examines
the legal effects of these various relationships during the currency of the
relationship. The consequences of an intimate adult relationship terminating,
whether by choice or by death, are discussed in Ch.11.

Personal consequences

Name
The principle that, "any person in Scotland may, without leave of the Court
call himself what he pleases" (*Johnston, Petitioner* (1899)) applies to both
men and women, with the caveat that the choice of name will fall foul of
the law if it is used for a fraudulent purpose. It follows that the practice
whereby some married women adopt their husband's last name on marriage
is no more than a social convention. Spouses, civil partners and cohabitants
may change their last names, or not, as they wish.

Residence
Actions of adherence and the husband's right to choose the place of the
matrimonial home were abolished by the Law Reform (Husband and Wife)
(Scotland) Act 1984 (ss.2(1) and 4, respectively). Each spouse, civil partner
or cohabitant has an equal right to decide where they should live.

Children
Marriage is of less significance for fathers than it used to be since non-
marital fathers who register as such (or re-register if registration was before
4 May 2006) now acquire parental responsibilities and parental rights in
respect of their children automatically, just like mothers and married fathers
(Children (Scotland) Act 1995 s.3). Once the Adoption and Children

(Scotland) Act 2007 s.14, comes into force, civil partners and cohabiting couples will be eligible to adopt a child in the same way as married couples.

Re-partnering

A person cannot marry or register a civil partnership while he or she is already in either kind of formal relationship (Marriage (Scotland) Act 1977 s.5(4)(b); Civil Partnership Act 2004 s.86(1)(d)). Once the existing relationship is dissolved by divorce, dissolution or the death the other spouse or civil partner, individuals are free to enter a new formal relationship. While a spouse or civil partner is not prevented from cohabiting with someone other than his or her existing partner, such a relationship will almost certainly be grounds for divorce or dissolution. Where a couple's relationship is one of simple cohabitation, either party may cohabit with, or enter a marriage or civil partnership with, a third party.

Sexual relations

Incurable impotence makes a marriage voidable and wilful refusal to have sexual relations may justify divorce. Adultery is a ground for divorce. While lesbian and homosexual relations do not amount to adultery, such conduct will almost certainly justify the non-participating spouse in seeking a divorce. At one time, the law took the view that a husband could not rape his wife, but that absurd notion has long since been dismissed (*S v H.M. Advocate* (1989)). The legal system avoids acknowledging the sexual dimension of civil partnership, so there is no scope for a voidable Scottish civil partnership. Sexual infidelity by a civil partner would almost certainly justify dissolution on the behaviour ground. Since cohabitation may be terminated at will, sexual (mis)conduct is not relevant for that purpose.

Domicile and habitual residence

Domicile, the link between an individual and a legal system, can be particularly important for personal purposes like the capacity to marry or register a civil partnership and succession to moveable property. Increasingly, ordinary or habitual residence is now used as the connecting factor for civil purposes. Marriage no longer has any effect on a person's domicile (Domicile and Matrimonial Proceedings Act 1973 s.1) and has no effect on habitual residence. Neither civil partnership nor simple cohabitation ever had any such effect.

Nationality and immigration

While marriage and civil partnership have no automatic effect on either partner's nationality, the foreign spouse or civil partner of a British citizen can acquire nationality by naturalisation more easily than can other persons, based on residence for three years (British Nationality Act 1981 s.6). Cohabitation has no effect on nationality. Marriage and civil partnership are important for immigration purposes, with foreign spouses, civil partners, fiancé(e)s and intending civil partners gaining entry more easily than is the case ordinarily. While these rules do not apply to cohabitants, they are admitted on a discretionary basis. Nationals of Member States of the European Economic Area and their spouses or civil partners are not governed by these rules and can enter and stay in the United Kingdom more easily.

CONTRACT AND DELICT

Contract

A host of sexist common law provisions, including the husband's guardianship of a young wife, the presumption that a wife was her husband's domestic manager (and, thus, his agent) and the husband's liability for his wife's ante-nuptial debts, were abolished by the Law Reform (Husband and Wife) (Scotland) Act 1984. The Family Law (Scotland) Act 1985 sums up the present law thus:

"marriage or civil partnership shall not of itself affect . . . the legal capacity of those parties or partners" (s.24(1)(b)).

Consequently, spouses and civil partners have the same contractual capacity as all other people.

However, the decision in *Smith v Bank of Scotland* (1996) and its vast progeny place an important qualification on that general rule. In *Smith,* a wife had granted a standard security to the bank over the matrimonial home, which she co-owned with her husband, so that he could obtain additional finance for his troubled business. When the bank sought to realise the standard security, she alleged misrepresentation and undue influence by her husband. The bank's failure to advise her to seek independent legal advice was central to her ultimate success in having the standard security reduced. Obviously, banks are now more careful to give the requisite advice, but anyone dealing with a spouse, civil partner, cohabitant or, indeed, other relative, in the context of cautionary obligations, should exercise considerable care.

Delict

At common law, spouses could not sue each other in delict, partly because the spouses were viewed as one, but also because such an action would not usually bring an overall financial benefit to the family unit. Statute intervened (Law Reform (Husband and Wife) Act 1962 s.2(1); Family Law (Scotland) Act 2006 Sched.3)) and spouses can now sue each other as if they were strangers, as can civil partners and cohabitants. There is no automatic liability for the delictual conduct of a significant other.

One spouse may claim damages in respect of the death of the other for loss of support, distress and anxiety caused by contemplating the deceased's suffering prior to death, grief and sorrow caused by the deceased's death, the loss of the deceased's society and guidance, and funeral expenses (Damages (Scotland) Act 1976 s.1). In addition, the surviving spouse may claim for loss of the deceased's services (Administration of Justice Act 1982 s.9). Quite separately to any claim he or she may have, a surviving spouse may also be the deceased's executor. If the deceased survived the delictual event and died later as a result of his or her injuries, the deceased's right of action now transmits to his or her executors, who may raise an action for damages or continue any action the deceased had time to raise (Damages (Scotland)

Act 1976 s.2A). Where a spouse or partner is injured and survives, recovery is also possible for services rendered to the injured person by a partner or relative as a result of the injuries sustained and to compensate for services which the injured person can no longer provide to a partner or other relative (Administration of Justice Act 1982 ss.7–9). These rights were extended first, to different-sex cohabitants who were living with the deceased "as husband or wife" immediately prior to the deceased's death (Administration of Justice Act 1982 s.14(4)), then to civil partners (Civil Partnership Act 2004 Sched.28) and finally, to different-sex cohabitants who were living together "as civil partners" (Family Law (Scotland) Act 2006 Sched.2).

PROPERTY

The general position
At common law, on marriage, a husband became the owner of virtually all of his wife's moveable property and administrator of her heritable property. For this reason, ante-nuptial marriage contracts were popular amongst the wealthy. From the mid-nineteenth century, statute whittled away at the husband's dominant role. The current position is that,

"marriage or civil partnership shall not of itself affect the respective rights of the parties to the marriage or as the case may be the partners in a civil partnership in relation to their property" (Family Law (Scotland) Act 1985 s.24(1)(a)).

Thus, as a general rule, spouses and civil partners are treated like strangers when it comes to property. This was always the position for cohabitants. However, this general rule is subject to a number of qualifications. The fact that two people are in an intimate relationship can have an impact on their property, since spouses and civil partners (but not cohabitants) are obliged to aliment each other. On divorce or civil partnership dissolution, a whole separate legal regime applies to property division. On the death of one spouse or civil partner, the survivor has certain succession rights, with more limited rights being available to cohabitants. Perhaps the most striking exception to the use (but not ownership) of property lies in the treatment of the family home, a matter discussed at the end of this chapter. In addition, the law recognises that couples will often arrange their lives differently from strangers and lays down a number of presumptions about the ownership of certain kinds of property.

The presumptions
The Family Law (Scotland) Act 1985 created two presumptions about the ownership of the most common household property. It should be remembered that these are simply presumptions and they can be rebutted by evidence. Where specific property falls outwith the presumptions, disputed ownership will fall to be resolved according to the ordinary rules of property.

The presumptions are as follows:
- *Household goods*. The 1985 Act created a presumption that household goods are owned by the spouses in equal shares and this was later

extended to civil partners (1985 Act s.25(1)). "Household goods" are defined as goods "kept or used at any time during the marriage or civil partnership in any family home for the joint domestic purposes of the parties", but money and securities, domestic pets and cars and other road vehicles are specifically excluded (1985 Act s.25(3)). The presumption applies to goods "acquired in contemplation of or during a marriage or civil partnership". However, it does not apply to goods acquired "by way of gift or succession from third parties" and so, for example, wedding presents given by friends will be outside its ambit. A similar presumption now applies to cohabitants who are living together as spouses or civil partners (Family Law (Scotland) Act 2006 ss.25 and 26).

- *Savings from housekeeping allowance.* Where a dispute arises over the ownership of "any allowance made by either party for their joint household expenses" or property derived from such an allowance, the money or property is treated as belonging to each party in equal shares, unless the parties have made an agreement to the contrary (1985 Act s.26). Thus, assuming nothing is said, where one civil partner buys a lottery ticket with some of the housekeeping allowance, any winnings belong to both partners in equal shares. Again, a similar presumption now applies to cohabitants who are living together as spouses or civil partners (Family Law (Scotland) Act 2006 ss.25 and 27).

ALIMENT

Each spouse or civil partner owes an obligation to aliment the other (Family Law (Scotland) Act 1985 s.1(1)). The extent of the obligation is to provide such support as is reasonable in the circumstances, having regard to:
- the needs and resources of the parties;
- the earning capacities of the parties;
- generally, to all the circumstances of the case (s.4(1)).

In Ch.5, we saw that these criteria applied to the obligation to aliment a child and the same principles apply, with allowance being made for the fact that adults are generally more able to provide for themselves. A party's conduct is irrelevant unless it would be "manifestly inequitable" to ignore it (s.4(3)(b)). Claims for aliment are competent even where the parties are living in the same household (s.2(6)), although it is a defence to a claim that they are so doing and the defender intends to continue to support the pursuer in this way (s.2(7)). Where the parties are no longer living together, the defender may offer to receive the pursuer into his or her own household and provide aliment there. Such an offer only constitutes a good defence where it would be reasonable to expect the claimant to accept the offer to be housed in the defender's household and, in particular, the court is directed to have regard to "any conduct, decree or other circumstances" (s.2(8) and (9)). When considering a spouse's or civil partner's claim for aliment, the court enjoys the same powers as it has when dealing with aliment for children (s.3). It should be noted that the obligation to aliment a spouse or civil partner terminates on divorce or civil partnership dissolution when the law on financial provision becomes relevant. There is no alimentary obligation between cohabitants.

CRIMINAL LAW AND JUDICIAL PROCEEDINGS

Criminal law

As a general rule, the criminal law treats spouses and civil partners like strangers and, thus, one spouse can steal from the other (*Harper v Adair* (1945)) and a husband can rape his wife (*S v H.M. Advocate* (1989)). Special measures are available to combat the problem of domestic abuse, although these are in addition to the possibility of prosecution for assault under the ordinary criminal law.

Adult relationships may be particularly relevant to specific offences. Bigamy is an obvious example, since it is committed where a married person goes through a second ceremony of marriage while the first marriage is still in existence. Where marriage, civil partnership or cohabitation brings a person into a quasi-parental relationship with a child, the law recognises the potential for sexual exploitation of the child. Thus, the Criminal Law Consolidation (Scotland) Act 1995 provides that it is an offence for a step-parent or former step-parent to have sexual intercourse with a step-child or former step-child, in certain circumstances (s.2). Non-marital cohabitants are covered by an offence relating to intercourse where the adult was in a position of trust in respect of the child (s.3).

Giving evidence—criminal cases

One spouse is a competent witness against the other in criminal proceedings; that is, he or she may give evidence (Criminal Procedure (Scotland) Act 1995 s.264(1)). However, a spouse cannot be compelled to give evidence, unless that spouse was the victim of the alleged crime or was injured by it (1995 Act s.264(2)(a)). Nor can a spouse be compelled to disclose any communication made between the spouses during marriage (1995 Act s.264(2)(b)). Neither the prosecution nor the defence may comment upon a spouse's failure to give evidence (1995 Act s.264(3)). Similar provisions apply to civil partners (Civil Partnership Act 2004 s.130). Cohabitants are both competent and compellable witnesses against each other. The special protection against compellability, afforded to spouses and civil partners, is currently under review and may be removed in the future.

Giving evidence—civil cases

While there is some debate on the matter, it is probably the case that spouses are both competent and compellable witnesses against each other in civil proceedings, subject to an exemption in respect of marital communications (Evidence (Scotland) Act 1853 s.3). While it is competent for a spouse to give evidence relating to whether sexual intercourse took place between the couple, he or she cannot be compelled to do so (Law Reform (Miscellaneous Provisions) Act 1949 s.7(2)). Former spouses do not appear to be protected from giving evidence against each other, in the civil context, nor are civil partners or cohabitants.

THE MATRIMONIAL OR FAMILY HOME

At common law, one result of the separate property rule was that, where a spouse owned or was the sole tenant of the home, he could evict his partner at will (*Millar v Millar* (1940)). During the 1970s, increased attention focused on the problems of domestic abuse and how the law could be improved to protect the victims. Resulting from the work of the Scottish Law Commission (*Report on Occupancy Rights in the Matrimonial Home and Domestic Violence* (1980)), the Matrimonial Homes (Family Protection) (Scotland) Act 1981 sought to address these problems. The 1981 Act does not affect ownership of the home but, rather, is concerned with the use of it. Initially, it applied to married couples and, to a more limited extent, to different-sex cohabitants. Civil partners benefit from parallel legislation (Civil Partnership Act 2004 Part 3) and the 1981 Act has been extended to same-sex cohabitants (Family Law (Scotland) Act 2006 s.34). The protection offered by the 1981 and 2004 Acts applies during the relationship and ceases to have effect on divorce or civil partnership dissolution, when the law on financial provision becomes relevant. Other legislation is designed to combat abusive behaviour in the context of personal relationships, more generally (see particularly, the Protection from Harassment Act 1997 and the Protection from Abuse (Scotland) Act 2001).

What is a "matrimonial or family home"?

A matrimonial or family home includes obvious residences, like houses or flats, as well as caravans or houseboats, where the home "has been provided or has been made available by one or both of the spouses [or civil partners] as, or has become, a family residence" (1981 Act s.22; 2004 Act s.135(1)). It includes ground or buildings attached to the home itself and "required for the amenity or convenience" of the home, like a garden. It does not matter which of the spouses or civil partners acquired the property, or when, and a couple can have more than one such home, for example, a flat in town and a cottage in the country. Any home acquired by one spouse or civil partner for his or her own use is not included under the Acts. The Family Law (Scotland) Act 2006 amended the1981 and 2004 Acts to clarify certain ambiguities. As a result, a home provided for one spouse or civil partner to live in separately from the other, whether with or without the children, is not a matrimonial or family home. Similarly, where tenancy in a home is transferred from one party to the other and the home is occupied by the transferee, the home ceases to be a matrimonial or family home.

"Entitled" and "non-entitled" spouses and civil partners

Central to the 1981 Act is the concept of "entitled" and "non-entitled" spouses. An entitled spouse is one who has a right to occupy the matrimonial home, whether because he or she is the owner or tenant or because he or she is allowed by a third party to occupy it (s.1(1)). A spouse with no such right is a "non-entitled" spouse. Thus, where the wife bought the home and it has been used by the couple, she is the entitled spouse and her husband is the non-entitled spouse. Parallel definitions apply to civil partners (2004 Act ss.101 and 135(1)).

Occupancy rights

The 1981 and 2004 Acts gives the non-entitled spouse or civil partner the right to live in the home by providing that, if already living there, he or she has the right to continue to occupy it (1981 Act s.1(1)(a); 2004 Act s.101(1)(a)), or, if not, to enter and occupy it (1981 Act s.1(1)(b); 2004 Act s.101(1)(b)). These rights can be exercised along with any child of the family or a child treated as such (1981 Act s.1(1A); 2004 Act s.101(7)). A non-entitled spouse or civil partner may renounce his or her occupancy rights but only in a particular home (i.e. there cannot be a blanket renunciation for all future homes), and the renunciation must be in writing and sworn before a notary (1981 Act ss.1(5) and (6); 2004 Act ss.101(5) and (6)). Where there has been no cohabitation between the parties for a period of two years and the non-entitled spouse or civil partner has not occupied the home during that time, occupancy rights are lost (1981 Act ss.1(7) and (8); 2004 Act s.101(7) and (8)). This is subject to a "stop the clock" provision, whereby no account is taken of the period of time between the lodging of an application for a regulatory order or an exclusion order and resolution of the application (1981 Act s.9A; 2004 Act s.111A).

Subsidiary and consequential matters

Simply having the right to live in the home might not be enough on its own and, for example, a landlord would be unlikely to permit continued occupation where the rent remained unpaid for some time and a home without any appliances or furniture would be of limited use. For the purpose of securing his or her occupancy rights, the non-entitled spouse or civil partner is allowed to do a number of things, like paying the rent or mortgage and carrying out essential repairs, without the permission of the entitled party (1981 Act s.2(1); 2004 Act s.102(1)). The court may make an order apportioning expenditure between the spouses or civil partners in respect of such payments (1981 Act s.2(3); 2004 Act s.102(3)). In addition, the court may authorise non-essential repairs and apportion payments made in respect of them (1981 Act s.2(4); 2004 Act s.102(4)).

Regulatory orders

Either spouse may apply to the court for an order regulating occupancy rights and associated matters. This part of the Act applies not only where there is a non-entitled and an entitled spouse or civil partner, but also where the parties are both entitled or permitted to occupy the home. A regulatory order may:

- declare the applicant's occupancy rights;
- enforce the applicant's occupancy rights;
- restrict the non-applicant's occupancy rights;

- regulate the exercise of occupancy rights by either party (1981 Act s.3(1); 2004 Act s.103(1)).

The court is bound to declare occupancy rights, where they exist, but has discretion in granting the remaining orders. In exercising its discretion, the court is directed to make such an order as appears "just and reasonable having regard to all the circumstances of the case, including:"

- the conduct of the spouses or civil partners in relation to each other and otherwise;
- the respective needs and financial resources of the spouses or civil partners;
- the needs of any child of the family;
- the extent (if any) to which, (i) the matrimonial home, and (ii) any relevant item of furniture and plenishings, is used in connection with a trade, business or profession of either spouse or civil partner; and
- whether the entitled spouse or civil partner offers or has offered to make available to the non-entitled spouse or civil partner any suitable alternative accommodation (1981 Act s.3(3); 2004 Act s.103(3)).

As we shall see, these criteria are used again later in the 1981 and 2004 Acts. In addition, the court cannot make an order under these provisions where its effect would be to exclude the entitled spouse or civil partner from the home since exclusion orders are dealt with elsewhere in the statutes (1981 Act s.3(5); 2004 Act s.103(5)).

Exclusion orders
The right to live in the home is of little value if the threat of domestic abuse continues because the abusive partner is also living there. For this reason, the 1981 Act introduced the exclusion order, which empowers a court to order a person to leave the matrimonial or family home, regardless of his or her rights as owner, tenant or non-entitled spouse or civil partner. The court is directed that it,

> "*shall* make an exclusion order if it appears that the making of such an order is *necessary* for the protection of the applicant or any child of the family from *any conduct or reasonably apprehended conduct* of the non-applicant spouse [or civil partner] which is or would be *injurious to the physical or mental health* of the applicant or child" (1981 Act s.4(2); 2004 Act s.104(2), emphasis added).

However, the court is also directed not to grant an exclusion order if it would be unjustified or unreasonable, having regard to all the circumstances of the case, including those set out in s.3(3) of the 1981 Act and the parallel provisions in the 2004 Act (1981 Act s.4(3)(a); 2004 Act s.104(3)(a)).

Initially, judicial hostility to the 1981 Act meant that it was interpreted in a very restrictive way (*Bell v Bell* (1983)), but the courts overcame these early problems and are now more willing to exclude an abuser from his or her home. Perhaps the clearest guidance on how the court should approach an application for an exclusion order was given by Lord Dunpark, when he said that the court should consider the following questions:

"1. What is the nature and quality of the alleged conduct?

2. Is the court satisfied that the conduct is likely to be repeated if cohabitation continues?

3. Has the conduct been or, if repeated would it be injurious to the physical or mental health of the applicant or to any child of the family?

4. If so, is the order sought necessary for the future protection of the physical or mental health of the applicant or child?" (*McCafferty v McCafferty* (1986), p.656).

Protection of occupancy rights against dealings

The value of occupancy rights would be greatly diminished if the entitled spouse or civil partner could sell the home to a third party and the third party could then come along and evict the non-entitled spouse or civil partner. For this reason, the 1981 and 2004 Acts contain provisions designed to protect against such dealings with third parties. The non-entitled party's rights under the Acts cannot be prejudiced by the entitled party's dealings with the property (1981 Act s.6(1)(a); 2004 Act s.106(1)(a)). Nor can a third party acquire a right to occupy the property as a result of such dealings (1981 Act s.6(1)(b); 2004 Act s.106(1)(b)). However, no protection is offered against certain dealings, where, for example, a third party purchaser, acting in good faith, obtains an affidavit from the seller, declaring that the subjects of the sale are not a matrimonial or family home in which the seller's partner has occupancy rights (1981 Act s.6(3); 2004 Act s.106(3)). This, combined with the fact that occupancy rights cease after two years non-cohabitation and non-occupation, can result in injustice to a non-entitled party (*Stevenson v Roy* (2002)).

Protection where both spouses are entitled to occupy the home

Increasingly, spouses who buy their homes do so in joint names and it can be anticipated that many civil partners will act similarly. This means that there is neither an entitled, nor a non-entitled, party. Each will have the right to live in the home and neither can bring an action of ejection against the other (1981 Act s.4(7); 2004 Act s.104(7)). However, the court can still regulate occupancy and grant exclusion orders. Where each spouse or civil partner has a *pro indiviso* share in the property he or she can sell or mortgage his or her share and can apply for a decree of division and sale in order to force the sale of the whole property. However, the Act restricts the effects of such action. Where one spouse or civil partner sells his or her share in the home to a third party, the occupancy right of the other will not be affected, nor will the third party acquire a right of occupancy (1981 Act s.9(1); 2004 Act s.109(1)). While one spouse or civil partner may still apply for a decree of division and sale, the court has discretion to refuse the decree, to postpone it, or to grant it subject to conditions (1981 Act s.19; 2004 Act s.110). In reaching its decision, the court is directed to consider all the circumstances of the case, including the factors set out in section 3(3) of the 1981 Act or section 103(3) of the 2004 Act, as appropriate, the conduct of the parties, and whether the party bringing the actions has offered suitable alternative accommodation to the other.

Tenancy transfer orders

Many spouses and civil partners are joint tenants in their home while, in other cases, only one is the tenant. In either case, the court can regulate occupancy or grant an exclusion order. In addition, it can transfer the tenancy from one to the other (1981 Act s.13(1); 2004 Act s.112(1)) or, where both are tenants, vest the tenancy in one of them alone (1981 Act s.13(9); 2004 Act s.112(10)) and provide for reasonable compensation to be paid to the deprived former tenant (1981 Act s.13(11); 2004 Act s.112(12)). In reaching its decision, the court is directed to consider all the circumstances of the case, including the factors in section 3(3) of the 1981 Act or section 103(3) of the 2004 Act, as appropriate, the applicant's suitability to become a tenant and the applicant's capacity to perform the obligations under the lease (1981 Act s.13(3); 2004 Act s.112(3)). A copy of the application must be served on the landlord who must be given an opportunity to be heard before the court grants the transfer (1981 Act s.13(4); 2004 Act s.112(4)), although the court can transfer tenancy even where the landlord does not agree (1981 Act s.13(6); 2004 Act s.112(7)). Certain kinds of tenancy, like a tied house, cannot be transferred by the court (1981 Act s.13(7) and (8); 2004 Act s.112(9) and (11)).

Matrimonial (and similar) interdicts

In order to offer further protection against domestic violence, the 1981 Act took the traditional remedy of interdict, whereby the court orders a person not to do a particular thing, and "gave it teeth", through a power of arrest empowering a police office to arrest a person without a warrant where there was reasonable case to suspect breach of (civil) interdict (1981 Act ss.15–17). Parallel provisions were created in respect of civil partners (2004 Act ss.113–117). With the passing of the Protection from Abuse (Scotland) Act 2001, offering another version of interdict and power of arrest, what was on offer became unnecessarily complex and the Family Law (Scotland) Act 2006 repealed the relevant provisions in the 1981 and 2004 Acts.

"Matrimonial interdicts" – and their civil partnership equivalent – remain competent even where the spouses are living together (1981 Act s.14(1); 2004 Act s.113(1)). They seek to restrain or prohibit specific conduct by one spouse or civil partner towards the other or a child of the family (1981 Act s.14(2)(a); 2004 Act s.113(2)(a)). In certain circumstances, such an interdict may also prohibit a spouse or civil partner from entering or remaining in a matrimonial or family home (but only if ancillary to an exclusions order); any other residence occupied by the applicant; any place of work of the applicant; or any school attended by a child in the permanent or temporary care of the applicant. (1981 Act s.14(2)(b); 2004 Act s.113(2)(b)). A power of arrest may be attached to such an interdict, now under the 2001 Act.

Cohabiting couples

The 1981 Act originally applied to "a man and woman who are living with each other as if they were man and wife" and now extends to same-sex partners who are living together as if they were civil partners (s.18(1)). In determining who qualifies, the court is directed to consider all the circumstances of the case including the duration of the cohabitation and whether there are any children of the relationship or who are treated as such (s.18(2)). However, there are important differences between the way the Act applies to married couples and civil partners, on the one hand, and to cohabitants, on the other. The latter have no automatic occupancy rights and must apply to the court to be granted them. Initially, these may be granted for a period of up to six months and, thereafter, any number of extensions of up to six months each may be granted (s.18(1)). Where both partners are entitled to occupy the home, there is no need to apply for occupancy rights and the Act applies as if such rights had been granted (s.18(3)). Where the partners have occupancy rights, most of the provisions of the Act can be used by them. For example, they can apply for regulatory orders (s.3), exclusion orders (s.4) and tenancy transfer orders (s.13). "Domestic interdicts" are the cohabitants' equivalent of matrimonial interdicts (s.18A). The protection against dealings afforded to spouses and civil partners does not apply in the case of a cohabitant (s.18(5)).

Debt, sequestration and the family home

Debt enforcement in Scotland has had a colourful history in the recent past with a flurry of legislation in the early part of this century. The relevant legislation will be touched on only in brief outline here and reference should be made to specialist texts. Poinding and warrant sales are now a thing of the past with the primary method of debt enforcement being the debt arrangement scheme (Debt Arrangement and Attachment (Scotland) Act 2002 and the extensive regulations made thereunder). While a debtor is participating in the scheme, a creditor being paid under it is precluded from executing any form of diligence against, or from seeking the sequestration of, the debtor (2002 Act s.4). However, attachment of the debtor's goods kept in the home is permitted in respect of "non-essential assets", in exceptional circumstances, and after a sheriff has granted an exceptional attachment order (2002 Act s.647(1)). Since the list of "essential assets" is extensive, moveable property needed by the family for ordinary life is protected.

Where the debtor has been charged to pay a debt exceeding £3,000 and the period for payment has expired without payment being made, land attachment is the current route by which a creditor can seek to sell the debtor's heritable property (Bankruptcy and Diligence (Scotland) Act 2007). Clearly, this poses a threat to the family home. However, the creditor must go through a lengthy procedure before seeking warrant to sell the property and, even then, the court retains extensive discretion to refuse to grant warrant, to defer it or to suspend its effect for up to a year. In exercising this discretion the fact that the property is the sole or main residence of the debtor or family members, including a spouse, civil partner or cohabitant, is central.

The family home receives special protection in the context of bankruptcy under section 40 of the Bankruptcy (Scotland) Act 1985. The 1985 Act contains its own definitions which are not identical to those found in the 1981 Act and should be consulted for its terms. Essentially, it provides that the trustee in sequestration may not sell a family home without the consent of the debtor's spouse or civil partner (or former spouse or civil partner, if he or she is occupying the family home) or the permission of the court. The court may refuse the application, grant it subject to conditions or postpone the granting of it for up to a year.

Further reading:
E. E.Sutherland, *Child and Family Law*, 2nd edn (W. Green, 2008), Chs 13 and 14.

---

10. DIVORCE AND CIVIL PARTNERSHIP DISSOLUTION

Divorce has been available in Scotland from the time of the Reformation, with adultery and desertion being the only grounds mentioned in the Act of 1573. Later statutes extended the grounds but, despite the addition of the no-fault ground of incurable insanity, in 1938, divorce remained firmly tied to the concept of fault, and only the "innocent spouse" could raise the action in respect of the other grounds. It was not until the Divorce (Scotland) Act 1976 that the concept of no-fault divorce gained meaningful recognition, with divorce being notionally available on the basis of "irretrievable breakdown". In reality, the 1976 Act created a mixed system, combining fault (adultery, behaviour and desertion) and no-fault (non-cohabitation for two years with spousal consent and for five years). The magnitude of the reform should not be underestimated, however, since, for the first time, couples who agreed that divorce was the correct solution for them were freed from the need to rake over past misdeeds. The Gender Recognition Act 2004 added a new ground of divorce. The advent of civil partnership brought with it the need to provide for dissolution of these new marriage-equivalents for same-sex couples and a system, almost identical to that for divorce, was put in place.

The Scottish Law Commission recommended modest reform of the grounds for divorce in 1989, essentially, shortening the periods of non-cohabitation required for the no-fault grounds from two and five years to one and two years, respectively, abolishing desertion as a ground for divorce and removing certain defences (*Report on Reform of the Grounds of Divorce* (1989)). These recommendations were finally implemented by the Family Law (Scotland) Act 2006, amending the 1976 Act, and extended to civil partnership dissolution.

This chapter will concentrate on divorce and conclude with a brief note on civil partnership dissolution since it can be anticipated that the latter will be statistically less common, in Scotland, for some time to come. Just as they required no formalities to enter their relationship, cohabitants need not go through any formal procedure to end it. However, they may still have to resolve disputes over the future arrangements for their children and over money and property and may become involved in judicial proceedings in order to do so.

JUDICIAL SEPARATION

Judicial separation has long been a remedy available to an unhappy spouse and, while distinct from it, may be granted on any of the grounds that would justify divorce on the basis of "irretrievable breakdown" (1976 Act s.4, referring to s.1(1)(a)). It was more widely used in the past, when divorce was more difficult to obtain and was less socially acceptable. While it gives a judicial stamp of approval to the parties' separation, it does little to alter their legal position and, most significantly, does not free them to remarry. Despite the Scottish Law Commission's recommendation that it be abolished (*Report on Family Law* (1992)), judicial separation has been retained as a remedy for spouses and has been extended to civil partners (Civil Partnership Act 2004 s.120).

DIVORCE

The Divorce (Scotland) Act 1976 provides that the court may grant decree of divorce in two situations. The first is where the marriage has broken down irretrievably (s.1(1)(a)) and the second is where an interim gender recognition certificate has been issued (s.1(1)(b)). Gender recognition will be discussed first, before irretrievable breakdown is explored.

Gender recognition

As a result of two decisions of the European Court of Human Rights (*Goodwin v United Kingdom* (2002) and *I v United Kingdom* (2003)), the Gender Recognition Act 2004 was passed. The Act lays down the procedure whereby an adult (s.1(1)) in the UK may have his or her "acquired gender" (being other than that indicated on the person's birth certificate) recognised and recorded. Where the application is successful, a single applicant receives a full gender recognition certificate and "the person's gender becomes for all purposes the acquired gender" (s.9(1)). Where the applicant is married or a civil partner, he or she receives only an interim gender recognition certificate and must obtain decree of divorce or civil partnership dissolution prior to the full certificate being issued (s.4(3)).

For this reason, a new ground of divorce was introduced. A court may grant decree of divorce where an interim gender recognition certificate has been issued to either party to the marriage (1976 Act s.1(1)(b)). While either party may raise the action, it is anticipated that this will usually be done by the applicant for gender recognition and the court granting the decree of divorce must also issue a full gender recognition certificate at the same time (2004 Act ss.5(1)(b)). Where the couple wish to continue their relationship, they may simply cohabit or they may register a civil partnership and there is an expedited procedure to enable them to do the latter. This enabled the whole procedure to pass muster before the European Court of Human Rights (*R and F v United Kingdom* (2006)).

Irretrievable breakdown
The Divorce (Scotland) Act 1976 provides that the other ground on which decree of divorce will be granted is that the marriage "has broken down irretrievably" (s.1(1)(a)). This, apparently simple, approach is misleading in two respects. First, irretrievable breakdown can only be established by satisfying one of the four (formerly five) factual circumstances set out in the Act (s.1(2)). Thus, if spouses cannot satisfy one of the four factual circumstances, they cannot get divorced, however irretrievable they believe the breakdown to be. Secondly, provided that the pursuer can establish one of the four factual situations, he or she will be entitled to decree, even if the marriage might be salvaged; that is, it has not broken down irretrievably. It is hardly surprising, then, that the four factual situations themselves have come to be known as the "grounds for or of divorce".

Grounds for divorce
Each of the four grounds of divorce is discussed below. Proof of each ground is on the balance of probabilities (1976 Act s.1(6)). For completeness, it should be noted that the defence of collusion, being "an agreement to permit a false case to be substantiated or to keep back a good defence," was abolished by the Family Law (Scotland) Act 2006 s.14. The fact that the defender has a religious objection to divorce is not a ground for refusing the decree (*Waugh v Waugh* (1992); *Taylor v Taylor* (2000)).

Adultery
Irretrievable breakdown will be established if "*since the date of the marriage the defender has committed adultery*" (s.1(2)(a)). Adultery is voluntary sexual intercourse with a person of the opposite sex who is not one's spouse. It is not adultery for a spouse to form a close association with a person of the opposite sex unless sexual intercourse is involved, nor does a lesbian or homosexual affair qualify. It is not adultery for a woman to have donor insemination without her husband's consent (*MacLennan v MacLennan* (1958)). Since the act must be voluntary, a woman who is raped does not commit adultery (*Stewart v Stewart* (1914)), although a married rapist does. A good faith belief that one's spouse is dead is no defence to an action for divorce based on adultery (*Hunter v Hunter* (1900)).

The following defences apply in the context of adultery:
- Lenocinium (s.1(3)). This occurs where the pursuer actively and seriously encourages the defender to commit adultery and this

encouragement was the cause of the adultery (*Hunter v Hunter* (1883), per Lord President Inglis at p.365).

- Condonation (s.1(3)). Essentially, condonation arises where the pursuer knows of the adultery and continues to live with the defender, and amounts to legal forgiveness. The 1976 Act encourages couples to attempt reconciliation and, thus, a period of resumed cohabitation of up to three months is permitted without the defence of condonation arising (s.2(2)). In addition, where the court believes there is a prospect of reconciliation and continues the case, no resumption of cohabitation during that time will bar an action for divorce (s.2(1)).

Behaviour

Irretrievable breakdown will be established if "*since the date of the marriage the defender has at any time behaved (whether or not as a result of mental abnormality and whether such behaviour has been active or passive) in such a way that the pursuer cannot reasonably be expected to cohabit with the defender*" (s.1(2)(b)). Only behaviour after the marriage is relevant and a single act (e.g. of violence) may suffice. The behaviour can be active or passive and, while a person's condition may be involuntary, it may result in behaviour which is such that the pursuer cannot reasonably be expected to cohabit with the defender. Thus, where a person suffers from bi-polar disorder, with the result that he stays in bed and shows no interest in the family, the conduct may qualify, if it has sufficient impact on his or her spouse (*Fullarton v Fullarton* (1976)). The behaviour itself need not be reprehensible, since it is the effect it has on the pursuer that is relevant. So, for example, driven commitment to one's career may be applauded in some circles, but it may also result in divorce (*Taylor v Taylor* (2000); *cf. Ross v Ross* (1997)). Similarly, a do-it-yourself enthusiast who reduced the family home to a building site for two years, with the intention of improving it, justified his wife in seeking a divorce (*O'Neill v O'Neill* (1975)). Nor need the conduct be directed at the other spouse (*White v White* (1966)). Behaviour is the most flexible of all the grounds for divorce and may include the following: physical, verbal or economic abuse; neglectful conduct or indifference; certain kinds of sexual behaviour; obsessive behaviour; drunkenness or drug abuse; and certain kinds of criminal conduct.

There are no specific provisions on resumed cohabitation or reconciliation attempts, in the behaviour context, although the court could continue the action where it believed there was the prospect of reconciliation, and resumed cohabitation during this period would not bar the action for divorce (s.2(1)).

Non-cohabitation for one year and the defender's consent

Irretrievable breakdown will be established if "*there has been no cohabitation between the parties at any time during a continuous period of one year after the date of the marriage and immediately preceding the bringing of the action and the defender consents to the granting of the decree of divorce*" (s.1(2)(d)). It will be remembered that the two-year non-cohabitation period required under the original 1976 Act was reduced to one year by the Family Law (Scotland) Act 2006 s.11. The Act helps to establish what is meant by non-cohabitation when it provides that, "the parties to a marriage shall be held to cohabit with one another only when they are in fact living together as man and wife" (s.13(2)). In most cases, the couple will have separate homes. However, two people may be living under the same roof and yet not cohabiting, provided that they are not living together as husband and wife and such factors as the time they spend together, the nature of their relationship, financial arrangements and the absence of sexual relations, will be relevant. In one English case, the court accepted that the couple were not cohabiting when the wife allowed her sick husband to return to the family home and helped to care for him, despite the fact that she continued to share a bedroom with her lover (*Fuller v Fuller* (1973)).

The non-cohabitation must be for a continuous period of one year but, again, reconciliation attempts are encouraged, and no account is taken of periods of resumed cohabitation not exceeding six months in all for the purpose of attempting reconciliation (s.2(4)). Resumed cohabitation during court-ordered continuation aimed at reconciliation is not subject to any time limit (s.2(1)). Again, no such period of time counts towards the year of non-cohabitation (s.2(4)).

In addition to non-cohabitation, the defender must consent to decree of divorce being granted. The defender can use consent as a bargaining tool, for example, to gain a financial advantage in the divorce. As Lord Maxwell put it, "it is perfectly open to the defender to withhold consent for any reason he thinks fit or for no reason" (*Boyle v Boyle* (1977), p.69). As far as the future arrangements for children are concerned, the court is bound to reach its decision having regard to their welfare but, sadly, that may not always prevent the parties from using the giving of consent as a negotiating tool in private discussions about the future arrangements for children.

Non-cohabitation for two years

Irretrievable breakdown is established if *"there has been no cohabitation between the parties at any time during a continuous period of two years after the date of the marriage and immediately preceding the bringing of the action"* (s.1(2)(d)). It will be remembered that the five-year non-cohabitation period, required under the original 1976 Act, was reduced to two years by the Family Law (Scotland) Act 2006 s.11. This ground of divorce is very similar to that providing for divorce after non-cohabitation for one year, but there are two important distinguishing features. First, and fairly obviously, the period of non-cohabitation required is two years. In computing the two years, the same periods of resumed cohabitation are permitted as were discussed in respect of one-year non-cohabitation (s.2(1) and (4)). The second difference between the two grounds is that the defender's consent is not required in this case. The original 1976 Act provided that a court was not bound to grant decree in respect of this ground "if in the opinion of the court the grant of decree would result in grave financial hardship to the defender" (s.1(5)). That defence was abolished by the Family Law (Scotland) Act 2006, s.13.

Desertion no longer a ground
For completeness, it should be remembered that one of the grounds for divorce under the original 1976 Act was desertion for two years (s.1(2)(c)). A parallel desertion ground applied to civil partnership dissolution (Civil Partnership Act 2004 s.117(3)(b)). With the reduction of the period of non-cohabitation required for the second of the no-fault grounds of divorce from five years to two, there was no longer any need to retain the desertion ground and it was abolished by the Family Law (Scotland) Act 2006 s.12 (divorce) and Sch.3 (civil partnership dissolution).

Postponing the granting of decree where a religious impediment to remarriage exists
In a very small number of cases and despite obtaining decree of divorce, an individual will not feel free to remarry until he or she completes a further step required by the rules of a particular religion. Judaism provides a good example since, in order to satisfy both civil and religious law, a person requires both decree of divorce and a religious divorce, know as a *get*. Obtaining a *get* requires the consent of both spouses. As the law stood prior to the recent amendment, a party could take advantage of the civil consequences of divorce while restricting his or her spouse's freedom to remarry by refusing consent to the *get*. In the attempt to address this problem, the Family Law (Scotland) Act 2006 s.15, added a new s.3A to the Divorce (Scotland) Act 1976, empowering a court to postpone the granting of a decree of divorce based on irretrievable breakdown of marriage where it would be "just and reasonable", and the applicant would be prevented from entering a particular kind of religious marriage until the other spouse does something to remove an impediment to such a marriage. Where it has granted a postponement, the court may recall it and, prior to doing so, may require the non-applicant party to produce a certificate from a relevant religious body confirming that the step necessary to remove the impediment has been taken.

The procedure
Both the Court of Session and the sheriff court have jurisdiction to grant divorce, although most actions are raised in the sheriff court (Court of Session Act 1830 and Divorce Jurisdiction, Court Fees and Legal Aid (Scotland) Act 1983 s.1). Only one of the parties to a marriage can raise an action for divorce and both parties must be alive when decree of divorce is granted. The Lord Advocate has the right to intervene in the public interest in any divorce proceedings, although this is rarely done. Where it is alleged that the defender committed adultery with a named person, the action must be intimated to that person, who has a right to intervene in order to deny the averments of adultery. Divorce cases involving children may also require intimation to relevant third parties, like the local authority if it is looking after the child. Where any order is sought in respect of the child under s.11 of the Children (Scotland) Act 1995,

the action must be intimated to the child, using a special form of notice, although intimation can be dispensed with by the court. Where a request has been made for the transfer of property, under s.8(1)(aa) of the Family Law (Scotland) Act 1985, the action must be intimated to any creditor with security over the property.

At one time, the pursuer and a witness had to appear in court before a divorce could be granted. The ordinary procedure is still available and is used where the divorce itself, or some ancillary matter, like the arrangements for children or property, is in dispute. However, the vast majority of divorces proceed by way of either the affidavit procedure or the "do-it-yourself" procedure.

Ordinary procedure

The initial writ, which sets out the pursuer's case and the remedies being sought, must be served upon the defender and other interested parties. If the defender does not intend to defend the action, it will normally proceed under the affidavit procedure. If the defender intends to defend the action or any aspect of it, he or she must intimate this to the court and lodge defences, usually within 21 days (the *induciae*). If the divorce is based on one year non-cohabitation with consent, the defender must intimate consent. The court can hear any preliminary motions to deal with such matters as sisting the action, interim residence and contact, or interim aliment. Like any civil action, an options hearing will be fixed to deal with various procedural and other matters.

Proof in divorce cases is on the balance of probabilities (s.1(6)). Corroboration is no longer required in civil proceedings (Civil Evidence (Scotland) Act 1988 s.1(1)), although, in establishing a ground of divorce, evidence from someone other than a party to the marriage is required (1988 Act s.8(3)), except when the do-it-yourself procedure is being used (1988 Act s.8(4) and (5)). As with other civil proceedings, hearsay evidence is permitted provided that the party who made the statement would have been a competent witness (1988 Act s.2(1)).

If the divorce involves a dispute in respect of children, two additional points should be noted. The first is confined to the sheriff court, and raises the possibility of an additional step in the proceedings, known as the child welfare hearing (Ordinary Cause Rules, r.33.22A). These hearings were introduced in 1996 in the attempt to resolve disputes involving children more quickly, provided that this can be done in a manner consistent with the child's welfare. The idea here is to gather the disputing parties together and see if some or all of the disputed matters can be resolved without the need for a full proof. A child welfare hearing will be arranged automatically if there is any dispute over the future arrangements for the children and, in any case, can be ordered by the sheriff at any time, at his or her own instance. The parties, including any child who has expressed the wish to be present, must attend in person, except on showing cause why this is not possible, and all parties are obliged to provide the sheriff with sufficient information to enable him or her to conduct the hearing. The sheriff then seeks to ensure the resolution of the disputed matters and takes a more interventionist role than is usually the case in court proceedings. If the dispute is not resolved, it will proceed to proof. The second point to note is that, where parental responsibilities and rights are in dispute in the divorce action, the court may refer the dispute on that point to a mediator accredited to a specified family mediation organisation at any stage (OCR, r.33.22).

At the end of defended proceedings the court grants a decree of divorce, if the pursuer is successful, or a decree of absolvitor if the defender is successful, thus rendering the matter *res judicata*. If the action has not been defended and the pursuer has not proved his or her case, the court grants a decree of dismissal.

Affidavit procedure
Where the action is not defended, the affidavit procedure can be used and this means that there is no need for the pursuer or the witnesses to appear in court (OCR, r.33.28). While not as cheap as the do-it-yourself procedure, it is less expensive than an ordinary proof. Unlike the do-it-yourself procedure, the affidavit procedure can be used for any of the grounds of divorce. The action begins in the same way as the ordinary procedure, with the initial writ being drafted and served upon the defender. Upon expiry of the *induciae*, the sworn affidavits of the pursuer and at least one witness are then submitted along with other relevant documents and a minute signed by the pursuer's solicitor. The court can then grant decree and the date of divorce is the date when the granting of the divorce appears in the rolls of court.

Simplified or "do-it-yourself" procedure
Where the divorce is based on either of the non-cohabitation grounds, there is a simplified procedure which enables spouses to obtain a divorce without the need to consult a solicitor at all (Divorce Jurisdiction, Court Fees and Legal Aid (Scotland) Act 1983 s.2). The applicant fills out a form, available from any sheriff court, and submits it to the court along with a copy of the marriage certificate, his or her statement sworn before a notary, and the prescribed fee. Where appropriate, the other spouse indicates consent by signing the form. Unfortunately, this cheap and simple procedure is restricted to a fairly narrow range of cases since it is only available where:
- the application is based on one of the non-cohabitation grounds;
- there are no children of the marriage under 16 years of age;
- neither party is seeking an order for financial provision;
- there are no other proceedings pending which could affect the validity of the marriage; and
- neither party suffers from a mental disorder.

A decree of divorce granted under this procedure cannot be reclaimed against.

Appeals and reclaiming motions
Appeals from the sheriff court are heard by the Court of Session and reclaiming motions from the Outer House of the Court of Session are heard

by the Inner House. Appeal to the House of Lords is possible, although rare. A decree of divorce takes effect immediately, although an extract decree of divorce will not normally be issued until the time for appeal has expired. Once an appeal has been lodged, the decree of divorce is suspended until the appeal is dealt with.

Registration
All divorces granted in Scotland on or after May 1, 1984 are registered in the Register of Divorces and an extract from the register can be obtained on payment of the prescribed fee.

CIVIL PARTNERSHIP DISSOLUTION
The Civil Partnership Act 2004 s.117, provides for dissolution of a civil partnership in all the same circumstances as justify the granting of decree of divorce, save for adultery. Arguably, the definition of adultery precludes its application to infidelity with a same-sex third party, but there was nothing to prevent the legislature creating a parallel concept covering this situation and sexual intercourse with a different-sex third party. Arguably, this is another example of Westminster's reluctance to acknowledge the sexual dimension of same-sex relationships. In practice, the omission is of no importance since infidelity would come within the ambit of the behaviour ground for dissolution. There is no civil partnership parallel to postponing decree of divorce where a religious impediment to remarriage exists since it is thought that there is no parallel problem. Decrees of civil partnership dissolution are registered in the Register of Dissolutions of Civil Partnership.

Further reading:
E. M. Clive, *The Law of Husband and Wife in Scotland*, 4th edn (W. Green, 1997), Chs 20–23 and 27
E.E. Sutherland, *Child and Family Law*, 2nd edn (W. Green, 2008), Ch.15

---

11. THE CONSEQUENCES OF TERMINATING INTIMATE ADULT RELATIONSHIPS

Intimate adult relationships terminate by choice or by the death of one of the parties. Divorce and civil partnership dissolution were discussed in the previous chapter and the legal aspects of death are discussed in Ch.2. There is extensive legal provision dealing with money and property in each case. In the past, where the parties cohabited outside marriage, they (or the survivor) had to rely on the general provisions of the law as it applied to strangers. In 1992, the Scottish Law Commission recommended modest changes in the way different-sex cohabitants were treated (*Report on Family Law*) and these were revisited subsequently (*Improving Scottish Family Law* (1999), *Parents and Children: A White Paper on Scottish Family Law* (2000) and *Family Matters: Improving Family Law in Scotland* (2004)). The Family Law (Scotland) Act 2006 implemented reform of the law for all cohabitants, albeit the reforms are of very limited compass.

As we saw in Ch.9, the personal consequences of marriage, civil partnership and cohabitation are fairly limited and, when the relationship ends, these effects generally terminate. Thus, a former spouse or civil partner is free to enter a new formal relationship, albeit there may be some restrictions in respect of step-children. What arrangements are made, either by the parents by the court, or by the CSA/C-MEC, for the future care and support of children, was discussed in Ch.5. Here our primary concern is with money and property from an adult perspective.

FINANCIAL PROVISION ON DIVORCE OR CIVIL PARTENRSHIP DISSOLUTION

The Family Law (Scotland) Act 1985, which resulted from the Scottish Law Commission's recommendations (*Report on Aliment and Financial Provision* (1981)), provides a regime for financial provision on divorce and the original Act has been amended to bring civil partners within its ambit. References in this section are to the 1985 Act, as amended, unless otherwise stated. One strength of the 1985 Act is that, for the first time, legislation sets out guiding principles, indicating what financial provision should seek to achieve, and provides the court with a broad range of orders it can make to give effect to these principles.

In an action for divorce or civil partnership dissolution, either party may apply to the court for financial provision and the general guidance given to the court is to make such orders as are both justified by the principles set out in s.9 of the Act and reasonable having regard to the resources of the parties (s.8(2)). As a general rule, the court is directed to take no account of the conduct of either party unless, "the conduct has adversely affected the financial resources which are relevant to the decision" (s.11(7)(a)). When it is considering the fourth (facilitation of adjustment) and fifth (alleviation of hardship) principles, it must disregard conduct "unless it would be manifestly inequitable to leave the conduct out of account" (s.11(7)(b)).

The guiding principles

The Act provides that financial provision on divorce or civil partnership dissolution shall be governed by the following principles.

Principle 1

The net value of the matrimonial or partnership property should be shared fairly between the parties to the marriage or civil partnership (s.9(1)(a)).

During the currency of the relationship, the general rule is one of separate property. On divorce or dissolution, the picture changes dramatically, with fair sharing of matrimonial or partnership property becoming the fundamental principle. As a general rule, fair sharing means sharing equally, subject to certain exceptions (s.10(1)). For this purpose, matrimonial property means all the property belonging to the parties or either of them at the relevant date (see below) which was acquired by them, otherwise than by way of gift or succession from a third party:

- before the marriage for use by them as a family home or as furniture or plenishings for such a home; or
- during the marriage but before the relevant date (s.10(4)).

Partnership property has an equivalent meaning (s.10(4A)). This very broad definition of property enables the courts to deal with almost everything acquired during the relationship, including what are often the largest assets the parties will have, like the home and pensions, as well as money, shares, cars and the like. It should be noted that the definition of matrimonial or partnership property here is not the same as the definition of household goods (Ch.9). Students sometimes get the two confused, with disastrous results.

The relevant date is whichever is the earlier of the date on which the parties ceased to cohabit or the date of the service of the summons in the action of divorce or dissolution (s.10(3)). Cessation of cohabitation is normally fairly easy to establish and, in cases of dispute, the court will look to the nature and circumstances of the particular relationship and determine a date (*Banks v Banks* (2005); *Bain v Bain* (2008)).

Anything acquired by the parties after the relevant date, usually the date of separation, is excluded from the pot of matrimonial or partnership property, as is property acquired by way of gift or succession from a third party. However, such property is not wholly irrelevant, since it will count as part of the individual's resources and, thus, become relevant when the reasonableness test is applied. So, for example, where the wife was given a flat by a third party, it was not matrimonial property, but it was part of her resources and was used to reduce the amount of capital to which she would have been entitled (*Buczynska v Buczynski* (1989)). In addition, while such property is not matrimonial or partnership property in its original form, if it is converted into other property, it loses its protected status. Thus, for example, when donated money was used to buy property, like a house, the house became matrimonial property (*Latter v Latter* (1990)). This apparent injustice is mitigated by the fact that the court has discretion to derogate from the general principle of equal sharing in certain circumstances and one such circumstance allows it to look at the source of the funds used to buy a particular asset (s.10(6)(b)).

Property is usually valued on the basis of net value at the relevant date. Net value is the value of the property after the deduction of certain permitted debts. In the past, a difficulty, known as the "Wallis trap", arose, particularly in relation to heritage, due to increasing property values between the relevant date and the action being disposed of. Where such an increase had occurred, the parties co-owned the property and one party obtained a property transfer order, he or she netted all the gain in value of the property (*Wallis v Wallis* (1992 and 1993)). Sometimes, the courts got around the resulting injustice by refusing to transfer the property and granting an incidental order for division and sale instead, thus enabling both parties to share in the increase in value (*Jacques v Jacques* (1995) and (1997)). The Family Law (Scotland) Act 2006 addressed the problem more squarely. It amended the1985 Act to provide that, where a court makes a property transfer order (but not any other order), the property is now valued at the "appropriate valuation date", being the date agreed by the parties, the date when the property transfer order is made or, exceptionally, a date "as near as may be" to the latter (s.10(3A)).

While matrimonial or partnership property should be shared fairly between the parties' and that usually means shared equally, the Act provides that it may be appropriate that property is shared "in such other proportions as are justified in special circumstances" (s.10(6)) and gives the following examples of what might amount to such special circumstances:

- The terms of any agreement between the parties on the ownership or division of any of the matrimonial or partnership property;
- The source of funds or assets used to acquire any of the matrimonial or partnership property where those funds or assets were not derived from the income or efforts of the parties during the marriage or civil partnership;
- Any destruction, dissipation or alienation of property by either party (*Bremner v Bremner* (2000));
- The nature of the matrimonial or partnership property, the use made of it (including use for business purposes or as a family home) and the extent to which it is reasonable to expect it to be realised or divided or used as security (*Trotter v Trotter* (2001));
- The actual or prospective liability for any expenses of valuation or transfer of property in connection with the divorce (*Sweeney v Sweeney (No.1)* (2004) and *(No.2)* (2005)).

In making an award under this principle, the court may order the payment of a capital sum, the transfer of property, and may make an order relating to a pension (ss.8(1) and 12(3)). It cannot make an order for the payment of a periodical allowance (s.13(2)).

Principle 2

Fair account should be taken of any economic advantage derived by either party from contributions by the other, and of any economic disadvantage suffered by either party in the interests of the other party or of the family (s.9(1)(b)).

Couples organise their lives in different ways and individuals make both economic and non-economic contributions, sometimes sacrificing their own economic position for the good of the other party or the family. This principle seeks to take account of the diversity of relationships. Economic advantage is "advantage gained whether before or during the marriage and includes gains in capital, in income and in earning capacity" and economic disadvantage is the reverse of that (s.9(2)). Contributions mean "contributions made whether before or during the marriage or civil partnership; and includes indirect and non-financial contributions and, in particular, any such contributions made by looking after the family home or caring for the family" (s.9(2)).

Advantages and disadvantages sustained, and contributions made, before the marriage or civil partnership began can be taken into account. So, for example, where a woman gave up a job to move to be with her future husband, that was taken into account in the subsequent divorce (*Dougan v Dougan* (1998)). Economic advantages and disadvantages are defined as widely as possible and have enabled the courts to take account of advantage gained, for example, by having housekeeping and child care provided or receiving money or unpaid labour for one's business. The disadvantage most often recognised is the loss of career opportunities, earnings and pension entitlement when a spouse or partner stays at home (*Louden v Louden* (1994)). The extent to which account can be taken of future losses or gains depends, to some extent, on whether they are speculative (*Dougan v Dougan* (1998)) or reasonably predictable (*Cahill v Cahill* (1998)).

In making an award under this principle, the court may order the payment of a capital sum and/or the transfer of property (ss.8(1) and 12(3)), but it cannot make an order for the payment of a periodical allowance (s.13(2)).

Principle 3

Any economic burden of caring, after divorce or civil partnership dissolution, for a child of the marriage or family under the age of 16 years should be shared fairly between the parties (s.9(1)(c)).

Children who have been raised in the parties' relationship in the past will need to be cared for in the future and caring for children has economic consequences. This principle seeks to share the future economic impact of child care between the parties. While the definition of which children are included here differs for spouses and civil partners, the overall result is much the same (s.9(1)(c) and 27(1)). Essentially, care of a child will be covered where the child is "a child of the marriage" or, in the case of spouses or civil partners, was an "accepted child". Clearly, this includes an adopted child and, frequently, it will extend to a step-child. In assessing the economic burden of child care, the court is directed to take a host of factors into account, including, for example, any award of aliment or child support liability and the child's age, health and educational needs. In addition, the court may take account of the fact that the payer is, in fact, supporting another person in the payer's household, whether or not there is any legal obligation to support that person (s.11(6)). The court is directed to disregard the conduct of either party, unless it has adversely affected the financial resources relevant to the decision (s.11(7)).

In making an award under this principle, the court may order the payment of a capital sum and/or the transfer of property and/or the payment of a periodical allowance (ss.8(1) and 13(2)).

Principle 4

A party who has been dependent to a substantial degree on the financial support of the other party should be awarded such financial provision as is reasonable to enable him or her to adjust, over a period of not more than three years from the date of the decree of divorce or civil partnership dissolution, to the loss of that support on divorce or dissolution (s.9(1)(d)).

While much of the 1985 Act is centred on the notion of a clean break divorce, it may be unrealistic and unreasonable to expect the spouse or civil partner who has been dependent on the other to become self-supporting immediately. Where the division of property under the first three principles would not provide sufficiently for adjustment, this principle may be used to do so. For example, Principle 4 can be used to provide a "buffer" while a spouse retrains to enable him or her to gain employment (*Wilson v Wilson* (1998)). In assessing what, if any, order to make for financial provision under this principle, the court is, again, given a list of factors to consider, including, for example, the claimant's age, health and earning capacity and his or her retraining plans. Again, the court may take account of the fact that the payer is, in fact, supporting another person in the payer's household, whether or not there is any legal obligation to support that person (s.11(6)). In applying Principle 4, the court is given greater latitude to consider conduct. The starting point is, as before, that only conduct that affected resources is relevant (s.11(7)). However, conduct can also be considered where it would be "manifestly inequitable to leave the conduct out of account" (s.11(7)(b)).

In making an award under this principle, the court may order the payment of a capital sum and/or the transfer of property, although it is more usual for it to order the payment of a periodical allowance (ss.8(1) and 13(2)).

Principle 5

A party who at the time of the divorce or civil partnership dissolution
seems likely to suffer serious financial hardship as a result of the divorce
or dissolution should be awarded such financial provision as is
reasonable to relieve him or her of hardship over a reasonable period
(s.9(1)(e)).

As we saw, Principle 4 envisaged a short-term period of adjustment to independence. Principle 5 addresses the issue of past dependence, but over the longer term, and, indeed, awards here have been made until the death or remarriage of the recipient (*Bell v Bell* (1988)). It is designed to accommodate the older spouse who has been dependent through a long marriage and should be seen as a last resort. Ideally, the other four principles should be used to ensure a just result. It may be some time before there is the opportunity to see how this principle plays out for civil partners. In assessing what, if any, order to make for financial provision under this principle, the court is, again, directed to consider a list of factors, including the claimant's age, health and earning capacity and the duration of the marriage or civil partnership. Again, the court may take account of the fact that the payer is, in fact, supporting another person in the payer's household, whether or not there is any legal obligation to support that person (s.11(6)). The extent to which the court can take account of either spouse's conduct, under Principle 5, is the same as that under Principle 4.

In making an award under this principle, the court may order the payment of a capital sum and/or the transfer of property, although it is more usual for it to order the payment of a periodical allowance (ss.8(1) and 13(2)).

Orders the court can make

The 1985 Act expanded the range of orders the court may make with the aim of enabling it to meet all eventualities. Either party may apply for one or more of the following orders.

- *An order for the payment of a capital sum to him or her by the other party to the action* (s.8(a)).

An order for payment of a capital sum can be made on the granting of the decree of divorce or civil partnership dissolution or within a period of time specified when the decree is granted (s.12(1)). A degree of flexibility can be built into an order to pay a capital sum by making the order effective from a specified future date or ordering payment by instalments (s.12(2) and (3)). So, for example, payment may be postponed until after the youngest child reaches 18 and the house has been sold and instalment payments are particularly appropriate where assets are tied up in a business which generates income. As a general rule, a capital award cannot be varied at a later date. However, where there is a material change of circumstances, either party can apply to the court to have the date or method of payment varied (s.12(4)).

- *An order for the transfer of property to him or her by the other party to the action (s.8(1)(aa)).*

Again, an order for the transfer of property can be made on the granting of the decree of divorce or civil partnership dissolution or within a period of time specified when the decree is granted (s.12(1)) and can be made effective from a future date (s.12(2)). Either party can apply to the court to have the date of the transfer of property varied on demonstrating a material change of circumstances (s.12(4)). Where a third party's consent is required before property can be transferred, as, for example, where a lender holds a standard security over the property, then the court cannot order transfer until the requisite consent has been obtained (s.15(1)).

- *An order for the making of a periodical allowance to him or her by the other party to the action (s.8(1)(b)).*

The court is directed only to make an order for the payment of a periodical allowance where orders for the payment of a capital sum or the transfer of property would be inappropriate or insufficient in the circumstances (s.13(2)(b)). In addition, a periodical allowance may only be provided for where it is justified by principles 3, 4 or 5 (s.13(2)(a)). Thus, the idea is that a periodical allowance should be the exception rather than the norm. An order for the payment of a periodical allowance can be made on the granting of the decree of divorce or civil partnership dissolution or within a period of time specified when the decree is granted (s.13(1)(a) and (b)). In addition, such an order can be made after the decree is granted, where no such order has been made previously, and there has been a change of circumstances (s.13(1)(c)). The order may be for payment for a definite or indefinite period or until the happening of a specified event (s.13(3)). On showing a material change of circumstances, an order for payment of a periodical allowance may be varied or recalled by the court (s.13(4)(a)) or an order for the payment of a capital sum or the transfer of property can be substituted for it (s.13(4)(c)). Variation or recall can be backdated and the court may order money already paid to be repaid (s.13(4)(b)). Where the payer dies, the obligation to pay a periodical allowance continues against the deceased's estate, but it is open to the deceased's executor to apply for variation or recall of the order on the basis of a change of circumstances (s.13(7)(a)). If the payee dies, remarries or registers a civil partnership, an order for periodical allowance ceases to have effect except in relations to any arrears due (s.13(7)(b)).

- *An order relating to pension benefits (s.8(1)(ba)).*

A pension entitlement will often be one of the biggest assets that a person has but the difficulty with pensions is that they may not be capable of being realised immediately and it may not be economically sensible to do so. The Pensions Act 1995 added this option to the court's powers in respect of pensions. The court can make an order against the trustees and managers of pension schemes requiring them to pay lump sums as directed by the court (e.g. to the former spouse) when they fall due (s.12A). The following conditions must be satisfied before a court may make such an order: the court must have made an order for the payment of a capital sum by a party to the marriage (the "liable party"); the liable party must have rights or interests in benefits under a pension scheme which are matrimonial property; and the benefits must include the payment of a lump sum either to the liable party or on his or her death (s.12A(1)).

Section 12A orders are subject to variation or recall at the instance of an interested party, where the liable party's liability has been discharged other than by payment by the trustees or managers of the pension scheme (s.12A(5)). A feature of pension schemes is that rights under them can usually be transferred to another scheme, often when the member moves jobs. To take account of this possibility, regulations require the trustees or managers of the first scheme to notify the trustees or managers of the new scheme of the section 12A order and the trustees or managers of the new scheme then become liable under the order (s.12A(6) and (8)) and the same procedure applies to subsequent transfers. The other party is also entitled to notice of any transfer of pension rights.

The Pension Act 2004 established the Pension Protection Fund to be administered by the Pension Protection Board to deal with the problem of an employer becoming insolvent and, thus, unable to meet pension scheme obligations. Where the Board takes over the assets and liabilities of a pension scheme, it pays compensation to members of the scheme. This compensation may constitute matrimonial or partnership property (s.10(5A)), but the court may not make a s.12A order in respect of it (s.8(4A)) and any order already made is recalled (s.12A(7A)).

- *A pension sharing order (s.8(1)(baa)).*

This is the more radical option added by the Welfare Reform and Pensions Act 1999 and it empowers the court to take the liable entitled party's pension entitlement, separating off a part of it into a distinct pension entitlement and giving this part to the other party. The other party thus acquires a pension entitlement that can be enhanced by further contributions. Again, where the Pension Protection Board has taken over the assets and liabilities of a pension scheme, the court may not make a pension sharing order in respect of matrimonial or partnership property consisting of compensation under the 2004 Act (s.8(4A)).

- *An incidental order (s.14).*

In order to ensure that the courts have the broadest possible range of powers, a number of incidental orders are provided for. Incidental orders are orders for financial provision and, as such, must be justified under the principles set out in s.9 and are subject to the limitation of being reasonable in the light of the parties' resources. They include orders for valuation or sale of property; orders in relation to the matrimonial home; and orders setting aside terms in ante-nuptial or postnuptial marriage settlements. Any of these orders, except those relating to the occupation of the matrimonial home and associated expenses, may be granted before, on or after the granting or refusal of a decree of divorce (s.14(1)).

- *An anti-avoidance order.*

Spouses and civil partners will often be reluctant to give a soon-to-be former partner any more than they have to and some will go as far as alienating property or trying to hide assets. The court has special powers to order disclosure of resources in divorce and dissolution proceedings (s.20). In addition, it is armed with wide discretionary powers to interdict, vary or set aside transactions aimed at defeating a claim for financial provision (s.18). An application for variation or setting aside of a transaction or interdict must be brought within a year of the claim for financial provision being disposed of and only a transaction or transfer which took place within five years preceding the claim for financial provision may be varied or set aside (s.18(1)). In order to be successful, it is for the challenger to establish that the transaction or transfer has had, or is likely to have, the effect of defeating, in whole or in part, any claim for financial provision (s.18(2)). Where a third party has acquired rights in property in good faith and for value, the court is directed not to make any order prejudicing such rights (s.18(3)). Similarly, the interests of a person deriving title from such a third party are protected. Where the court varies or reduces a transaction or transfer, it may include in any order it makes "such terms and conditions as it thinks fit and may make any ancillary order which it considers expedient to ensure that the order is effective" (s.18(4)).

Enforcement

Orders for financial provision can be enforced, within Scotland, using all the usual methods of debt recovery. Reciprocal enforcement within the United Kingdom is reasonably straightforward. Further afield, ease of enforcement depends on whether various international conventions apply.

Agreements on financial provision

Many couples faced with divorce or civil partnership dissolution will try to reach agreement on financial provision and it is highly desirable that they should avoid acrimonious and costly litigation. They may find it helpful to use the services of a mediator to assist in the process. As a matter of practice, the agreement should be as comprehensive as possible and each party should have received independent legal advice. Assuming that the couple reach agreement, they need do nothing further. However, it is common to record the terms of the agreement. Where the action is being pursued under the affidavit procedure or by ordinary proof, it is usual to present the agreement in a minute, or joint minute, of agreement and ask the court to interpone its authority to it. If the parties are using the do-it-yourself procedure, the agreement should be recorded in the Books of Council and Session.

While couples are encouraged to make their own financial arrangements, the court retains the power to set aside or vary an agreement, or any term of it, where it was not fair and reasonable at the time it was entered into (s.16(1)(b)). The court can exercise this power on granting decree of divorce, or within a time specified when the decree was granted (s.16(2)(b)). The whole circumstances of the agreement, including nondisclosure of information and the legal advice each party received, are relevant to assessing its reasonableness. In addition, the court has the power to vary or set aside an agreement in respect of a periodical allowance: where the agreement itself provides for such variation; where the payer has been sequestrated; or where a maintenance calculation has been made under the Child Support Act 1991 (s.16).

Claims by cohabitants

In the past, the legal system treated former cohabitants as strangers when their relationship ended. Occasionally, a former cohabitant might recover using other legal concepts, like unjustified enrichment (*Shilliday v Smith* (1998)), but there was no comprehensive legal provision. The Family Law (Scotland) Act 2006 now provides for a former cohabitant claiming financial provision after the cohabitation ends, but only in certain limited circumstances (*Fairley v Fairley* (2008)).

A claim is competent "where cohabitants cease to cohabit otherwise than by reason of the death of one (or both) of them" (s.28(1)). Thus, the claimant must have been "a cohabitant": that is, the parties must have been living together as if they were husband and wife or civil partners (s.25(1)) and the court is directed to have regard to the length of the cohabitation, the nature of the relationship and the nature and extent of any financial arrangements during that time (s.25(2)). The cohabitation must have ceased and it can be anticipated that this will be interpreted as it is for spouses and civil partners. However, it is of additional importance for a claim here since the action must be raised "not later than one year after the day on which the cohabitants ceased to cohabit" (s.28(8)) and the court has no discretion to extend this period of time.

The court may make the following orders:

- *An order for a capital sum (s.28(2)(a))*

The court is confined to making a capital award (whether on a specified date or by instalments: (s.28(7))) and to doing so in order to balance economic advantages and disadvantages sustained by one party in the interests of the other or a relevant child (s.28(3)–(6)). A "relevant child" here includes both a child of whom the cohabitants are parents and an "accepted" child, under the age of 16 in either case (s.28(10)).

- *An order in respect of any economic burden of caring for the couple's child after the cohabitation has ended (s.28(2)(b))*

The order here is not limited to payment of a capital sum and the court may order periodic payments. However, only a child under the age of 16 "of whom the cohabitants are parents" is covered and not an "accepted" child.

- *"such interim award as it thinks fit" (s.28(2)(c))*.

It should be noted that the court has no power to transfer property from one former cohabitant to the other, nor to make any of the orders relating to pensions that are available to spouses and civil partners. Cohabitants may opt out of claims for financial provision under s.28, subject to the ordinary rules on the validity of contracts, but not to the sort of challenge open to spouses and civil partners under the Family Law (Scotland) Act 1985 (ss.8 or 16). Where a person has both a qualifying cohabitant and a spouse or civil partner, he or she may face parallel claims for financial provision, with neither claimant having automatic priority.

SUCCESSION

The law of succession merits study in its own right and only the briefest outline will be provided here. When a person dies, his or her funeral expenses and outstanding debts must be met. Thereafter, what happens to his or her property depends on whether the deceased dies intestate or testate: that is, whether he or she left a will.

Intestacy

In cases of intestacy, the estate is distributed as follows.

Prior rights

The surviving spouse or civil partner is entitled to make three claims under this head covering: the dwellinghouse in which he or she was ordinarily resident up to the value of £300,000; furniture and plenishing therein, up to the value of £24,000; and financial provision of up to £42,000, if the deceased left descendants, or up to £75,000 if the deceased left no descendants. Where the deceased's estate exceeds the maximum value, the widow, widower or surviving civil partner is entitled to money in place of the dwellinghouse and must select which items of furniture and plenishings he or she wishes to claim (Succession (Scotland) Act 1964, ss.8 and 9).

Discretionary award to the surviving cohabitant of the deceased

See below.

Legal rights

After prior rights have been satisfied, legal rights may be claimed. They apply only to the remaining moveable estate and entitle the surviving spouse or civil partner to half of that, if the deceased is not survived by descendants, or one-third, if the deceased is survived by descendants. Any descendants share one-third of the moveable estate between them (1964 Act ss.10 and 11).

Division of the free estate

The remainder of the estate, known as the "free estate", goes to the first group of the deceased's relatives on the following list: children; parents and siblings (each share half between them); brothers and sisters; parents; widow, widower or surviving civil partner; grandparents; aunts and uncles (1964 Act s.2(1)).

Devolution of property if there is a will

Legal rights cannot be defeated regardless of what the deceased has provided for in his or her will. Thus, the surviving spouse or civil partner and any children will be entitled to claim legal rights from the deceased's moveable estate. If the deceased has failed to provide for any one of them, there is no problem. However, each individual provided for in the will must choose between the legacy and legal rights (1964 Act s.13). A person cannot claim both. Thereafter, the deceased's property is distributed according to the will.

Neither marriage nor divorce has the effect of revoking a prior will. Where property has been left to a "husband" or "wife", or a named person, described in that way, it is a matter of construction whether a former spouse is entitled to claim (*Henderson's Judicial Factor v Henderson* (1930); *Pirie's Trustees v Pirie* (1962)).

Claims by cohabitants

At common law, a surviving cohabitant had no right to succeed to his or her partner's estate on intestacy. The deceased may have made provision for the survivor in a will, but this did not (and still does not) displace the prior and legal rights of a surviving spouse, civil partner or children. The Family Law (Scotland) Act 2006 now provides that a surviving cohabitant may apply to a court for financial provision out of the estate of his or her deceased partner, but only in certain limited circumstances.

A surviving cohabitant may only apply if the deceased died intestate (or partially intestate) (s.29(1)(a) and (10)) and domiciled in Scotland (s.29(1)(b)(i)) (*Chebotareva v King's Executrix* (2008)). In addition, the couple must have been cohabiting immediately before the deceased's death (s.29(1)) and, as for financial provision when the parties split up, "cohabiting" means living together as husband and wife or as civil partners (s.25(1)(b)(ii)). An application must be made "before the expiry of the period of 6 months beginning with the day on which the deceased died" (s.29(6)). The court has no discretion to extend the period of time "for cause shown", nor can it award anything on the basis of the survivor's "reasonable expectations", as had been proposed by the Scottish Law Commission (*Report on Family Law* (1992)).

The court may only make an award to the survivor out of the deceased's "net intestate estate", being, what is left after the following have been met: inheritance tax, liabilities that take priority over legal rights and the prior rights, and legal rights and the prior rights of a surviving spouse or civil partner (s.29(2) and (10)). After these claims have been met and if there is anything left, the claim of a surviving cohabitant may be considered. Two points should be noted here. First, the survivor's claim takes precedence over those of other relatives, including the legal rights of deceased's children and any surviving spouse's or civil partner's claim in respect of the free estate. Secondly, the free estate aside, priority is given to a surviving spouse or civil partner regardless of how short that relationship was and how long the cohabitation.

Provided he or she qualifies as outlined above, the surviving cohabitant may apply to the sheriff court or the Court of Session (s.29(5)) for the following orders:

- An order for the payment to the survivor of a capital sum;
- An order transferring specified heritable or moveable property to the survivor; and
- "such interim order as [the court] think fit" (s.29(4)).

Where an award is made to the survivor, it must not exceed what he or she would have been entitled to had he or she been a spouse or civil partner (s.29(4)).

In exercising its discretion, the court must have regard to:

- The size and nature of the deceased's net intestate estate;
- Any benefit received (or to be received) by the survivor on, or in consequence of, the deceased's death *and* form somewhere other than the deceased's net estate;
- The nature and extent of any other rights against, or claims on, the deceased's net estate;
- Any other matters the court considers appropriate (s.29(3)).

Law reform
In 1990, the Scottish Law Commission made extensive recommendations for reform of the law of succession (*Report on Succession* (1990)), but very few of them have been implemented. While not undertaking a fresh, comprehensive review, the Commission consulted on a number of issues recently, most notably the position of surviving family members on intestacy and the possibility of the deceased disinheriting relatives (*Discussion Paper on Succession* (2007)). Thus, reform of the law on succession seems a distinct possibility in the near future.

Further reading:
E.M. Clive, *The Law of Husband and Wife in Scotland*, 4th edn (W. Green, 1997), Chs 24 and 30;
E.E. Sutherland, *Child and Family Law*, 2nd edn (W. Green, 2008), Ch.16.

INDEX